THE AUTHENTIC LEADER AS SERVANT (ALS)

ALS I COURSE 5
HEALING-CARE LEADERSHIP
Attributes, Principles, and Practices

SYLVANUS N. WOSU, Ph.D

THE AUTHENTIC LEADER AS SERVANT
ALS I COURSE 5
Healing-Care Leadership Attributes, Principles, and Practices

© Copyright 2024 by Sylvanus N. Wosu Ph.D.

Printed in the United States of America
ISBN: 978-1-959449-46-1

All rights reserved. No part of this book may be reproduced or transmitted in any form or by any means, electronic or mechanical, including photocopying, recording, or by any information storage and retrieval system, without permission in writing from the copyright owner.

Bible quotations are from the New King James (NKJV) version of the Bible unless otherwise indicated.

Other versions used in this book are the New International Version (NIV), New Living Translation (NLT), King James Version (KJV), English Standard Version (ESV), and Good News Translation (GNT). Unless otherwise specified, NKJV should be assumed.

The views expressed in this work are solely those of the author and do not necessarily reflect the views of the publisher, and the publisher disclaims any responsibility for them.

To order additional copies of this book, contact:
Proisle Publishing Services LLC
39-67 58th Street, 1st floor
Woodside, NY 11377, USA
Phone: (+1 646-480-0129)
info@proislepublishing.com

TABLE OF CONTENTS

FOREWORD	XI
ACKNOWLEDGMENTS	XV
DEDICATION	XVII
PREFACE	19
About Leader As Servant Leadership (LSL) Model	22
About the Authentic Leader as Servant (ALS)	25
About the ALS Courses	26

CHAPTER 1
UNDERSTANDING LEADERSHIP ATTRIBUTES — 35

- Functional Definitions — 35
- Comparisons With Other Works — 40
- Principle of Leadership Attribute — 42
- Authentic Leadership Attributes — 43
- Summary 1 Understanding Leadership Process — 49

CHAPTER 2
LEADERSHIP HEALING-CARE ATTRIBUTE — 53

- Principle of Healing-Care Attribute — 55
- Summary 2 Leadership Healing-Care Attribute — 56

CHAPTER 3
DEVELOPING WHOLENESS – SELF-HEALING — 61

- Characteristics of Healing-Care Attribute — 61
- Inviting God into the Healing Process — 63
- Developing a Sense of Oneness — 64
- Developing a sense of Self-worth in Healing — 64
- Developing a Sense of Purpose in Healing — 65
- Developing self-efficacy for the Healing — 65
- Summary 3 Developing Wholeness–Self-Healing — 66

CHAPTER 4
DEVELOPING THE ACTS OF HEALING-EMPATHY — 69

- Identify with State of Suffering and Infirmities — 69
- Summary 4 Developing the Acts of Healing-Empathy — 72

CHAPTER 5
DEVELOPING WHOLENESS-RECONCILIATION — 75
Total Forgiveness Drives Reconciliation — 76
Forgiving Others that Hurt You — 79
Acts of Forgiving Self — 80
Strategies for True Forgiveness — 81
Summary 5 Developing Wholeness-Reconciliation — 86

CHAPTER 6
DEVELOPING RELATIONAL WHOLENESS — 89
Managing Major Sources of Conflicts — 90
The Six Stages of Conflict Resolution — 91
Health Benefits and Effects of Forgiveness — 94
Pursue Reconciliation for Lasting Peace — 95
How to Achieve Reconciliation — 95
Humility as a Servant — 97
Summary 6 Developing Relational Wholeness — 101

CHAPTER 7
DEVELOPING THE ACTS HEALING-CARE COMFORT — 105
Sorrows that Need Comforting — 105
Strategies of Confronting Others — 106
Summary 7 Developing the Acts Healing-Care Comfort — 108

TOPIC INDEX — 113
REFERENCES — 115

Foreword

The modern world today is obsessed with standardization and modalities. As a result, in the realm of leadership, many books have spout associated leadership theories and models and explain them as the path to follow. However, the critical dimensions that distinguish the effectiveness of any leadership process are the values and attribute the leader brings to the table; desired change is influenced by leadership styles or standards. These many standards and theories of leadership often are not in step with the changing times or the followers' needs. The trend is a bit like stocking different kinds of foods in a grocery store and expecting that they will meet everybody's needs the same way and at all times. Aisles are packed with varieties of food with expiration dates in the future, but getting the best deal on the products is what really matters to those who buy and use the products

In many ways, this is the state of leadership in the modern world. Increasingly, even leaders of public institutions are tasked with turning a profit for themselves or the organization they serve. The idea of a "leader" seems to float uneasily alongside the ranks of fundraisers or profit raisers in contrast to any kind of role model for followers or employees. That which is knowable, measurable, and marketable has surpassed the difficult intangibility of strong moral leadership attributes as the central guideline for achievement and success.

In this complicated space, Dr. Sylvanus Wosu introduces his complex idea of the Leader as a Servant Leadership, which is in this book, modeled on Christian tradition. Like all intricate ideas, Dr. Wosu's central point depends on a paradox: a person is best qualified to lead when he or she is most ready to serve. This paradox has been monopolized rhetorically by "public servants" who often serve either self-interest or the interests of specific lobbies. The Authentic Leader as Servant penetrates past the superficial concept of "serving" and details the internal state of true servitude or Servanthood.

While the book is primarily focused on the Christian model of leadership attributes such as discipleship, empathy, affection, and Servanthood, it does so not merely on the grounds of blind faith, but rather via numerous contemporary sociological and business-driven studies on how leaders should seek a leader-follower relationship that is simultaneously productive and nurturing. Dr. Wosu's most piercing insights always involve this secular–Christian dialogue. This book demonstrates that Christ's model for leadership is one that may exist successfully outside the confines of a faith relationship; it places the values of Christ's religious significance in leadership at the center of the framework. It is clear from Dr. Wosu's generous own life story of faith—a faith tested by humbling difficulties—is at the center of both his orientation and motivation for writing.

In language that is so concise, it is often illustrated in mathematical formulas; Dr. Wosu explains the deep structural integrity of Christ's Leader as the Servant Leadership model. One could imagine leaders of any doctrine benefiting from the analyses contained in these pages. The book's message repeatedly encourages the reader to imagine a scenario or reflect on memories and personal experiences to prove or test its many points. Thus, the book depends on a form of praxis, a lesson that could be or has been enacted, by the participating reader. I am very impressed at the volume and level of thinking of the author. Parts of the book involve his personal story, which is especially riveting. I cannot imagine what he had to endure, which he referred to as a" wilderness walk," to accomplish the goal he set for himself. His life stories on these pages are inspiring and stimulating.

In this way, the text eschews dogmatism in favor of the self-discovery Socratic Method of teaching and learning. The reader is not badgered into complying with a religious objective but is rather asked to consider the applicability of difficult biblical concepts in relation to modern life. It is a fascinating and very thought-provoking read.

Hence, the book does not seek to make the leader a servant, a cookie-cutter corporate buzzword, but rather asks the reader to imagine him or herself interacting with a range of concepts. One of Dr. Wosu's great strengths is his reservation when it comes to forcing his reading's interpretation on the material he presents.

The book parallels Biblical and modern leadership scenarios in ways that consistently provoke thought, and while it is clear Dr. Wosu has his particular leadership style; the space for the reader's own thoughts is always left open.

The book could not have been written in any other way with integrity. Its format and formulas are offered to the reader of the leader as a servant role that it analyzes in its pages. To find a text that instructs from this humble position is profoundly refreshing in a genre that is often packaged inside a cover with a sizeable picture of the "modest" author, smiling egotistically beneath a name spelled out in large, gold lettering. Throughout its pages, this text feels as if it serves the reader.

In the end, this is the most satisfying aspect of the book. There is no standardized approach to achieving successful leadership. There is no promise of power and a bigger payday; in fact, the book often proffers just the opposite. The reader is not encouraged to devalue the experience of leadership by finding some economic metric for marking success but is rather asked to think deeply about the most basic elements of internal and social interaction within the framework of a Christian tradition. What this means will be different for every reader. Indeed, even in the context of single chapters, I found myself questioning or re-evaluating moments of my own life. This book serves; it doesn't feel like filling in multiple-choice questions, staring at a wall of flavorless grocery products, or hearing the endless servant promises of today's political scene. It feels like a humble invitation to consider a single paradoxical element of a profoundly productive tradition.

-Tobias Bates

Acknowledgments

A book on leadership attributes as aspects of Servant Leadership sprouted from the wealth of knowledge and the inspirations of many other leaders. Their writings were sources of inspiration, challenges, and examples of excellence to emulate.

Dr. Enefaa N. Wosu, my wife and life partner, for her love, commitment, and prayer support, especially during those long night hours I was not there for her and her constant reminder of who I must be as a leader-servant. Without her support, forbearance, wisdom, and encouragement, this project would not have been completed; I say, thank you very much.

And to God alone be all the glory and honor for the divine inspiration and guidance in initiating and completing this life-transforming book project.

Dedication

I humbly submit this book back unto the gracious hands of God who inspired the writings through His Holy Spirit!

I dedicate this book to my virtuous wife of 45 years, Rev. (Dr.) Enefaa Wosu whose spiritual leadership is an important gateway to our home, and to our four wonderful children—Prof. Eliada Wosu-Griffin EL, HeCareth, Tamuno-Emi, and Chidinma. From them all, I learnt what it meant to be a leader-servant. I could not be blessed with better teachers.

PREFACE

What characteristics did Biblical leaders like the Apostle Paul, Moses, Joshua, and Nehemiah as servants of their people display outwardly that distinguished them from other leaders, both then and now? The Apostle Paul kept his focus to *emulate* Christ and endured all the infirmities and persecutions he suffered to complete his goal to preach the gospel of Jesus Christ. He inspired Timothy and others through his effective *discipleship* leadership to imitate him as he emulated Christ. Moses' outward display of his *trust* in God's power earned him a good level of trust from the people and empowered him for the mission of delivery of God's children from bondage in Egypt; he had to *reproduce* himself in Joshua to complete the mission. But the greatest of them was Jesus Christ, who humbly sacrificed His life to finish the work of redemption. In His *Servanthood*, commitment, and love for the people, He became the ultimate *model* of a leader as a servant to *emulate*.

Let's consider for a moment secular leaders in these current times! For example, think of Henry Ford, who founded the successful Ford Motor Company; Bill Gates who created the global empire that is Microsoft; Albert Einstein, who in many ways is synonymous with a genius for his contributions to modern physics; Abraham Lincoln, remembered as one of the greatest presidents and leaders of United States; and many others like these we cannot mention. What did all these leaders have in common? What propelled them to turn their initial failures or challenges into eventual successes? None had a direct mentor or inherited any fortune from their parents. Nevertheless, they all eventually succeeded. These people can be distinguished from others based on their self-will to succeed, their self-confidence and belief in themselves, their self-determination, and their perseverance, among other characteristics. The distinguishing characteristics displayed externally in service or relationships toward others are the outward functional attributes that define that leader.

Think about yourself as a student, faculty member, or that new executive. What was it that made your journey to success different and even great? Students and colleagues, when they see or hear about my display of what I have referred to as the 'wilderness walk of faith', have asked me to share the critical attitudinal elements that made me remain inwardly resilient and undaunted and yet outwardly joyful in the difficulties I had faced. This book is the result of those reflections. Let me explain one such teaching moment.

Many years ago, sitting in my research lab on a Saturday morning trying to finish writing my dissertation, a fellow graduate student walked into the room to talk with me. He was contemplating terminating his graduate studies. He was a privileged single male student but felt the load was just too much.

"Sylvanus," he asked, with seriousness in his eyes, "your research advisor suggested that I should ask you, 'what is it that makes you tick?'.'What is it about you that makes you joyful and at peace with yourself and determined to finish, no matter the situations and high expectations we face in this department?"

What he asked me were deeply reflective questions, but I was willing and excited to answer them. Even so, before I do, let's look at the context. At that period in my life, I had four little children as a graduate student; in fact, more children than any of the faculties at that time, except for one faculty member who had eight children. I received little or no support from the department. I was then an international alien, did not qualify for financial aid, and was not given any research assistant position. I was, therefore, self-supported with two off-campus part-time jobs. I joked at being a minority of minorities, the only student in the department with such a label,—but I was self-willed to succeed. My adaptability attribute, coupled with perseverance and resilience, was all that I needed to succeed despite the odds against me. In every exam, homework assignment, or project I had to compete with students with full financial aid, plus they had nothing to distract their attention from their studies. I lived with the attitude that using disadvantages as an excuse was not an option. Aspiring to earn my Ph.D. was a life dream, and I was willing to give my ultimate best to actualize that dream even in the face of challenges. The choice was mine!

So I looked at my classmate and all I could see was a student striding through a valley through which I also walked. He needed me to show him how to walk the walk, to empathize with him. To answer his question, I smiled, not that I wanted to, but because it was just who I was. The joy he attributed to me was an overflow of my appreciation of God's grace that His life in me was externally manifesting His light to bless someone else. It was a great teaching moment; I capitalized on it to tell my classmate that my joy was not about me. He could see physically but about He who was in me, he could not see in the flesh; I needed him to know that I was just showing forth His life in me. At first, my classmate did not understand the spiritual prose or metaphor I was using. He looked surprised but open to hearing more.

I did not ask if he was a Christian. However, right on my desk was my small green pocket Bible. I opened to 2 Corinthians 12:9 (NIV) and handed it to him to read. As he read the passage: "But he said to me, 'My grace is sufficient for you, for my power is made perfect in weakness.' Therefore, I will boast all the more gladly about my weaknesses, so that Christ's power may rest on me," I noticed how absorbed he was in the words

He looked astonished and read it again, this time silently. "This is interesting, but what does this mean?" He asked. I took his question to mean, "How does this relate to my question?

I explained to my friend that the external attitudes he or my advisors saw in me that warranted the question, "What makes you tick" were inspired by my inner value system based on my faith in this same Christ and His teachings. My desire to manifest His life and self-confidence is all because of what He has promised in His word if I believed. I have believed His words and have gained self-determination and faith to make the right choices through Him for my life, and his spirit has given me perseverance and resilience to focus on finishing strong in pursuit of any goal. "With that faith, I have continued, more passionately and excitedly; I can look at my challenges and vulnerabilities and delight joyfully in them, even as an alien minority of minorities! His grace and power have empowered me to do all things I want to do. That is what makes me tick," I explained.

He looked at me as if he got his answer. "Wow, thanks!" he said, looking inspired and ready to face his challenges. As we concluded with a prayer, and he stood up to leave, I pointed empathetically to his face and said, "If I made it despite my challenges, you have absolutely no excuse but to persevere to complete your studies; you can make it too!"

It is fitting to report that this encounter with my classmate transformed his will and determination to continue. Yes, he was encouraged and went on to complete his graduate studies. He emulated self-will and perseverance from the example of the most vulnerable of all students in the department.

The inner value system of a Leader-Servant is founded not only on his faith but his self-will, coupled with self-leadership; it is the greatest mentor who can turn any situation into an inconceivable success. Self-will is the primary driver for determination, resilience, and perseverance. It is what wakes you up in the morning to ask for strength to do whatever it is you are setting out to do. Based on my life walk of faith, I can state with absolute certainty that faith is the unseen assuredness that can empower you to turn your life's probable impossibilities into great and improbable possibilities.

ABOUT LEADER AS SERVANT LEADERSHIP (LSL) MODEL

Looking at the testimony above, do you know the source that energizes the characteristics you display outside and how your inner self is related to what others see outside? What distinguishes you from others is what combines to define your attributes! As a follower, can you identify the characteristics that distinguish your leaders? As an executive, how do you base your evaluation of yourself? Or how do you evaluate that brand-new manager or new youth director you want to hire? To what do you compare the individual's qualities when you look at his CV? What is the basis of your measure? Do you know if you are a substantial leader? These personal questions and much more are the subjects of this two-volume book, 'The Authentic Leader as Servant Part I: The Outward Leadership Attributes, Principles, and Practices', is written in two parts; the second part 'The Leader as Servant Leadership Model. Part II'; deals with the Inner Strength Leadership Attributes, Principles, and Practices.

When we think about today's corporate greed, deepening divide between the haves and have-not, gridlock in political systems, conflicts and wars, high divorce rates, and the rich young ruler in the Bible, it is easy to agree that all these people share a few things in common: self-centeredness, pride, lack of compassion, and greed. There is a great need in today's suffering world for leader-servants who display leadership attributes. These attributes should be oriented toward selfless service to others. Indeed, our world is increasingly drifting away from global serving reality toward the self and apathy. The most credible message or model for a possible solution to this dilemma and the answer to several complex leadership questions can be found in the foundation of the ultimate leader-servant, Jesus Christ. This book defines the Leader as Servant Leadership attribute as the combined acts of two or more distinctive functional leadership characteristics exhibited in service and relationship toward others. There is no better time than now for a book that presents comprehensive and irrevocable facts and principles regarding how to develop effective attributes of the leader-servant.

The Leader as Servant Leadership Model

My first book on this subject, The Leader as Servant Leadership Model, explains that Jesus' servant leadership model is based on the notion of a Leader as a Servant and not on a Servant as Leader. There are four distinct differences between a Servant as Leader (Servant-leader) and the Leader as Servant (leader--servant) models. It is pertinent to highlight them here to connect to this book, Authentic Leader as Servant.

A Leader as Servant is a leader first. The leader–servant as a leader does not in the line of duty go projecting or lording his or her power and authority over others but is the person to lead the process of influencing desired changes in others through his humble example of being a servant or having a serviceable attitude toward others. He or she is a serving leader, not a lording leader. He leads as a servant by putting others' needs above his own needs and rights. Jesus emphasized the word "as" meaning that the leader (the Master) chooses to serve as a servant even though he is the leader. A leader–servant emulates Jesus, who gave up all rights, and emptied and expended Himself on His followers. He empowered them to become more like Him. A leader-servant is known as a leader first but is seen as a great leader by his humble attendant heart and acts of service to others. His greatness comes from his ability to put others above himself.

Leader as Servant is a Biblical Concept. The model or image of a humble serving leader motivated Jesus' disciples to see that if their master could do this for them, they must also be able to do it for others. Jesus clearly demonstrated the process of leader-as-servant leadership. In some cases, He chose to serve by leading when He wanted to create the image or model of the leader-servant in certain acts. In other cases, He chose to lead by serving, when he showed care and empathy toward the people and led the disciples to see empathy as a leadership attribute.

Leader as Servant is an Authentic Leadership Model to follow. The Leader as the Servant leadership model intentionally positions Jesus as an original model of a leader to follow.

He was serving His disciples to demonstrate that the process of becoming a great leader was earned through humble acts of service to others; He made them understand that He was empowering them to succeed Him as leader-servants through service to others. The result was an incomparable legacy of leadership that changed their communities. The fact that Jesus relinquished his rights or shared His power did not diminish His power and influence. In fact, his influence increased at least 11 X 100%, if we ignore the one case of Judas.

The Leader as Servant Transforms Organizational Culture. The proposed LSL model seeks to transform and sustain the community or organization by instilling key leadership values or "leadership presence" among followers or an organization's members. Change is sustained when everyone in the organization takes ownership of the change. Rather than focusing on leading more followers to be great followers who conform to the organizational culture, LSL seeks to lead and empower better leaders to be distinguished leaders and community builders.

There are four distinctions, which clearly differentiate many of the existing servants as Leader-based philosophies in relation to servant leadership from my LSL model. Even in the corporate or institutional worlds, there is nothing better than Jesus on which to base Servant Leadership. There is nothing more authentic and impacting than the servant leadership modeled by the life and teachings of Jesus Christ.

The LSL model uses exploratory questions, scenarios, and graphic visualizations to excite critical thinking in ways no other book on this subject has yet attempted. Several personal testimonies of my wilderness walk of faith with God are used to connect the reader to real-life experiences of the concepts discussed. The riveting effect is that the text engages and encourages the reader to walk through the experiences presented. The aim is to inspire the reader spiritually, mentally, and professionally with this far-reaching exposition on the subject of servant leadership.

ABOUT THE AUTHENTIC LEADER AS SERVANT (ALS)

The *Authentic Leader as Servant* argues that no leadership model is as authentic, other-centered, able to build communities, and productive and service-oriented as the model of our ultimate leader-servant, Jesus Christ. No source can provide a better point of reference than that provided in the Bible. Hence, this book aims to be more than just a text on leadership; it hopes to be a personal discovery for those who aspire to develop effective leadership attributes that grow leaders as servants who ultimately develop thriving other-centered communities. This book presents a comprehensive, biblically-based study regarding how to develop these attributes and how they are applied in a servant leadership process. In this biblical context and for clarity, Servant Leadership means *Leader-as-Servant Leadership*. A *leader-servant* refers to a *leader as a servant*, which is distinct from a servant-leader or servant as leader.

Leader as Servant Leadership attributes are shaped by the Leadership's Inner Value system, which consists of character, motivation, and commitment. The *Authentic Leader as Servant* is presented as a necessary resource to complement my *The Leader as Servant Leadership (LSL) Model*. The LSL model integrates a transformative leadership framework and interactive dimensions of Servant Leadership. Leader as Servant Leadership is a process in which a leader, in his leadership position, purposefully chooses to put others' rights and needs above his positional rights and personal needs. He then serves, enables, and empowers followers for growth that builds a thriving organization. The LSL model looks at the predominant Servant Leadership concepts and shares how they compare with biblical principles on how we should lead and be led.

ABOUT THE ALS COURSES

The three books, *LSL Model* and *The Authentic Leader as Servant* (Parts I and II), together demonstrate that with today's global visions to reach people of all races and cultures, now is the time for an authentic servant's heart of service. Those visions and the leadership processes are most effective with the appropriate leadership attributes centered more on people than on the organization, principles regarding how to develop effective attributes of leader-servant.

The ALS I and II combined presented twenty leaders as servant leadership attributes. The series of ALS courses supply training guide to understand, develop, and practice the attributes in a leadership process. Each course is independent and self-contained and does not depend on completing any other course in the series of 20 courses. It is, however strongly recommended, in fact a must read, that chapters 1 and 2 in each series be covered as they lay the foundation of LSL model on which ALS is based.

ALS (Parts I & II) Course Layout

The *Authentic Leader as Servant (ALS)* leadership (parts I and II) book has been broken down into 20 courses in workbook format to achieve three goals 1) Self-discovery of the acts of developing the attribute under review in the course, 2) deeper understanding of the principles, research and biblical teaching behind the attributes, and 3) Learning the strategies for practicing the attributes.

Instruction

The set of questions following each chapter are designed to serve as a guide to discover, explore, and practice the essential ALS leadership attributes, principles, and practices in leadership process. The questions are comprehensive review based on the content of this specific chapter only.

To maximize the learning outcomes, the learner must read through this chapter and sections. Some referenced scriptures in the book are repeated in the summaries for added review if needed, even though they were discussed in the section in which they apply.

> The exercises that follow each chapter will help you in not only understanding your own strength and weaknesses in your acts of the attribute but will guide you in developing practical strategies you can apply in self-leadership process or helping others grow in leadership
>
> All answers to the questions are contained in the associated chapter or sections; consultation of new sources, except for the reference scriptures, is not needed. Thus, it is expected that you answer the questions after you have read the associated section or chapter of the workbook. The scripture or other references cited are only for references as they already discussed in the book

---

ALS I Course 1: Affection Leadership Attribute—*Affection flows from a person to produce positive emotions for the well-being of another person.*

An average person will define the word "love" in the sense that affection is a characteristic of love. Nevertheless, that definition clouds the functional meaning of affection as an attribute of a leader-servant. Affection is a love action intentionally given to someone to create favorable emotion. We experience a positive emotion when we receive or give affection. In his acts of affection, the Apostle Paul communicated to the Corinthian Christians how he spoke to them freely with an open heart, because it was an important way to give affection (2 Corinthians 6:11-13). He also spoke of longing for them with the affection of Jesus Christ (Philippians 1:8); an affection that needs to be mutual (1 Peter 1:7). How is the affection leadership attribute an outward leadership attribute? This course explores this and other questions to discover the characteristics of affection attributes and to formulate a functional principle based on the expected outcome of affection and the effective use of these attributes in leadership.

ALS I Course 2: Discipleship Leadership Attribute- *Discipleship transforms and empowers followers for service leadership that grows communities.*

Discipleship as an act of developing a follower toward a specific goal is an important function of leadership to equip others to lead. *Discipleship transforms and empowers followers for service leadership that grows communities.* A disciple is a follower who willingly chooses to follow the master and submits to his discipleship and authority. In that regard, Jesus wanted all his followers to be his disciples and ambassadors because a disciple is always a follower. Organizationally, a follower could be a junior employee, any employee in a brand-new department, a new younger faculty, or just any person that needs to be guided through a journey of professional growth and good success. This course focuses on the general growth of followers through the acts of discipleship and presents the critical characteristics of discipleship as a leadership outward attribute. Functional definitions of leadership discipleship attributes and its principle will be presented based on those characteristics. Each characteristic will be discussed in detail with emphasis on strategies of how they can be further developed or practiced as a part of the servant leadership process.

ALS I Course 3: Emulation Leadership Attribute—*A great leader-servant outwardly and positively inspires a pattern of good works for others to follow.*

To emulate is to strive to be like someone else or to follow someone else's example by imitating something that inspires you about that person. This course evaluates how to learn from someone good leadership qualities to develop yours. How did you use what you learned from following the footstep of your hero to grow your leadership qualities. Jesus in the scripture modeled humility and Servanthood he wanted his disciples to develop same qualities. Emulation as a leadership attribute shares some characteristics with transformative leadership, where a leader intentionally conveys a clear vision of a goal, inspires the passion for the work toward the goal, and motivates the followers to follow. As a leader, how do you model a characteristic behavior for someone to follow or develop? How is Leadership Emulation Leadership Attribute an outward leadership attribute? This course explores this and other questions to discover the characteristics of affection attributes and to formulate a functional principle based on the expected outcome of effective use of these attributes in leadership.

ALS I Course 4: Generosity Leadership Attribute: G*enerosity is an outward measure of the level of sacrifice, what is shared, or the impact a giving makes, not just the size of the giving*

Generosity can be defined as "the *habit of giving* without expecting anything in return. It can involve offering time, assets, or talents to aid someone in need." Such habits can include spending your personal money, time, and/or labor for the welfare of others or expending (suffering or being consumed or spending) for others' well-being. When political leaders or Board members 'vote their conscience' on important issues that affect others, what is that "conscience" and how do such leaders contribute to the welfare of others? How can you, "Do all you can, with what you have, in the time you have, in the place where you are" for the betterment of humanity All giving to help humanity is crucial to help meet the needs of the most vulnerable of God's children, as demonstrated by God as attribute of God, In this course, we will explore what distinguishes a leader's act of giving from his inside intentions. The key leadership characteristics of generosity will be discussed with respect to Servant-Leadership generosity Attributes and Principles and the details how a leader-servant can develop those characteristics and then effectively practice service leadership.

ALS I Course 5: Healing-Care Leadership Attribute: *Comforting others in any trouble with the comfort with which God comforts us, brings healing-wholeness*

What is healing Care and what does it mean in practical terms to you as a leader? Effective leadership begins with an emotionally and spiritually healthy leader who can reconcile and bring comfort to the followers, irrespective of followers' feelings (good or bad) toward the leader. The healing attribute and personal security complement each other. You must have the capacity for self-healing and individual security if you are to meet others' comforts. Personal security provides the infrastructure to support leaders in adversity and heal others that are hurting. A leader's or a group's success is measured by the strength of the weakest member or follower in the group or team… Healing is one of the most abstract and least understood attributes in leadership, and yet one of the most important. The key distinguishing characteristics will be explored to formulate a working definition and principle of leadership healing-care attributes based on those characteristics. Each characteristic will be discussed in detail with emphasis on strategies of how they can be further developed or practiced by a leader-servant as part of the servant leadership process.

ALS I Course 6: Influence Leadership Attribute-*The true measure of leadership success in affecting desired change in conduct, performance, and relational connections in others is influence*

Leadership is an integrative process in which a person applies appropriate (leadership) attributes to guide and influence the desired attitudinal changes in others toward accomplishing a particular goal. Eight five percent of CEOs of top companies surveyed on their climb to leadership ladder said they were "influenced by another leader," compared to 10% and 5% for "natural gifting" and "result of a crisis," respectively. When we consider influence as a servant leadership attribute, we are talking about a distinguishing leadership characteristic that displays on the outside what a leader is inside, influence takes on a deeper meaning. In this course, the key leadership characteristics of influence will be identified and explored from research to frame definitions of the Servant-Leadership influence attribute and principle. Based on those characteristics, the key outcomes of effective leadership influence l how a leader-servant can develop those characteristics and then effectively practice service leadership.

ALS I Course 7: Persuasion Leadership Attribute—*The means of transforming others to a new perspective is through empathetic persuasion.*

Persuasion attribute affords the leader the capacity to convince his followers or others to believe and engage in a new idea or goal through encouragement rather than using his positional authority or intimidation. Because members of the group may already have their views on an issue, the leader must carefully approach persuasion as a learning process to avoid conflicts or polarizing the group. He must unify the diversity of views to get buy-in and willingness to agree and follow. The leader-servant primarily relies on making decisions within an organization based on persuasion rather than positional authority. In other words, you will never hear the Leader-servant say, "Do it because I am the boss, and I say to." This particular element offers one of the clearest distinctions between the traditional authoritarian model of leadership and the concept of Servant leadership. In this course, we will explore the technique of convincing rather than coercing as one of the most effective ways a leader-servant can build consensus within groups. Key characteristics of persuasion leadership attribute will be found, fully discussed, and modeled from the examples in the lives of other leaders.

ALS I Course 8: Reproduction Leadership Attribute—*Great leaders produce successors for legacy and greater courses as an expected product of an effective leadership reproduction.*

In his book, *360 Degree Leader*, John C. Maxwell says, "Great leaders don't use people so they can win. They lead people so they can all lead together." Such great leaders, like Jesus, Moses, Paul, and others developed other leaders through a process of reproduction. Is it possible for leaders of today to reproduce their vision in others so that can lead and build a legacy together? The answer to this question is of course yes. However, the effectiveness of a leader duplicating his leadership qualities in a follower depends on the leadership reproduction attribute of the leader. This course explores the distinguishing characteristics of reproduction as an outward attribute in servant leadership. Functional definitions of leadership reproduction attribute and its principle will be presented based on those characteristics. Each characteristic of reproduction attributes will be discussed in detail with emphasis on strategies of how they can be further developed or practiced by a leader-servant as part of the servant leadership process.

ALS I Course 9: Servanthood Leadership Attribute— *A leader-servant is most qualified to lead when ready to serve as a servant for the growth of others.*

The last time you engaged in a practical act of service on the job, at home, church, or in your community, what were the key elements in that act of service? Did you serve because you wanted to and chose to serve? Or was it because someone asked you to? The ultimate goal is for the leader's life to positively transform many lives in his or her community of followers. Consider the New Testament teachings of Jesus, who demonstrated the ultimate Leader as Servant Leadership. Jesus equated greatness to serving unpretentiously (humbly, as would a child), and He equated leading with choosing to serve others. That is the first affirmative test of authenticity for this attribute. What were the distinguishing characteristics that enabled you to serve? How is the Leadership Servanthood an outward leadership attribute? This course will give answers and meanings to these and personal reflective questions to discover the distinguishing characteristics of The Leadership Servanthood attribute. Functional definitions of The Leadership Servanthood attribute and principle will be provided based on the identified characteristics. Readers will benefit from numerous techniques, personal examples, empirical case study, and applications of the concepts.

ALS I Course 10: Trust-Integrity Leadership Attribute—*True leadership trust produces assured trustee's confidence and readiness to follow based on the credibility, competence, and shared relational connections of the trusted.*

A study examined more than 75 key components of employee satisfaction in top leadership and found that trust and confidence was the single most reliable predictor of employee satisfaction in an organization. This course will examine the results of the above study with respect to servant leadership, and how a leader-servant increases the satisfaction of the followers in an organization. When the organization is going through some challenges, how can a leader be credible in helping the followers understand the company's mission and strategy? How can he share information on how the company or institution, or department is doing and how the followers or employees will be affected? Suppose the organization's strategy is not aligned with its inner value or character, how does the leader build trust in followers or earn trust from them? Organizational leadership trust has been defined by as "an employee's willingness to take a risk for a leader with the expectation that, in exchange, the leader will behave in some desired way." The course will examine how the element of reliance and confidence in the actions of the trusted and organization are characterized by a combination of Competence (Can they do the job?), Benevolence (Do they care about me?), and Integrity (Are they honest?).

Referenced Scriptures

A variety of Bible translations from over 11,200 original Hebrew, Aramaic, and Greek words to about 6,000 English words do exist with variations in meanings and emphases. I am not a biblical scholar and do not pretend to be one; Hence, I have avoided researching the roots of these words and personally prefer New King James Version (NKJV). I have intentionally used other translations for three main reasons; first, to allow for increased impact and alignment of words to the most desired meaning and emphasis in the concepts being addressed. Second, I wanted new and personal discovery of meanings from translations with which I have not been familiar. And third, I wanted to allow readers who may desire translations other than the NKJV the benefit of their preferred translations. Hence, in addition to the NKJV, other translations used in the book include New International Version (NIV), New Living Translation (NLT), King James Version (KJV), English Standard Version (ESV), and Good News Translation (GNT). Unless otherwise specified, NKJV should be assumed.

Sylvanus Nwakanma Wosu

CHAPTER 1
UNDERSTANDING LEADERSHIP ATTRIBUTES

Leadership attribute is the combined acts of two or more distinctive functional leadership characteristics exhibited in service and relationship toward others.

The starting point of our discussion is the understanding of the key functional definitions and concepts that describe the theme of this book. In general, 1 will define leadership as an integrative process in which a person applies appropriate attributes to guide and influence the sought-after attitudinal changes in others toward accomplishing a particular goal. Specifically, the Leader as Servant Leadership is a process in which a leader intentionally chooses to put the follower's rights and needs above his positional rights and personal needs, and serves, enables, and empowers them for desired spiritual and professional growth that builds thriving communities.

FUNCTIONAL DEFINITIONS

In the context of these definitions, I will begin the descriptions of the leadership attributes of an authentic leader-servant by offering a functional definition of Leadership Attributes, and showing how that definition differs from those of Leadership Character, Characteristics, and Traits.

Leadership Character is the sum total of personal qualities in leadership, such as honesty, values, vision, trust, and so on that make up the moral capital of the leader; Leadership character should describe who the leader is inside or the leader's basic personality traits.

The Leadership Characteristics describe the distinctive characteristics or features of a leader, such as attitudes, competencies, skills, and specific experiences that go beyond his character (personality). Leadership characteristics determine how (through skills and competencies) the leader leads or take actions in the process of leadership in any particular situation;

The Leadership traits are the distinguishing leadership characteristics of a leader (these are things that define his leadership characteristics), which differentiate from personality traits... Leadership traits are the set of characteristics that define a particular leader's leadership. This means that a leadership characteristic is a trait when it is a unique characteristic of the leader.

Leadership Attributes, unlike leadership character, characteristics, and traits, is *a leadership attribute and the combined act of two or more distinctive functional leadership characteristics exhibited in service and relationship toward others* or traits externally displayed in action toward others. All leadership attributes grow out of the leadership inner value system but can be externally displayed predominantly as an outbound or outward attribute or both:

1. **Outbound Attributes:** These are distinctive outward-bound attributes emanating from the inner strength of the leader to support external conduct in service and relationships toward others. They form the internal core functional qualities that motivate or enhance the outward manifestation of the inside character toward others. The outbound attribute such as listening and vision, for example, are the direct results of the inner values of the leader such as patience, hearing, love, humility, or all the fruits of the spirit.

2. **Outward Attributes:** These are distinctive functional outward outer visible attributes emanating from the richness of the outbound and inner values of the leader. For example, external attributes such as Servanthood, emulation/modeling, empathy, etc. are outflows from the leader who will directly impact the follower. Outward attributes can be enriched by the outbound (inner) attributes. As shown in Figure 1, the outward attributes in general form the outer core of

functional attributes in the leader as servant leadership, but they can share some overlapping functions with the outbound attributes.

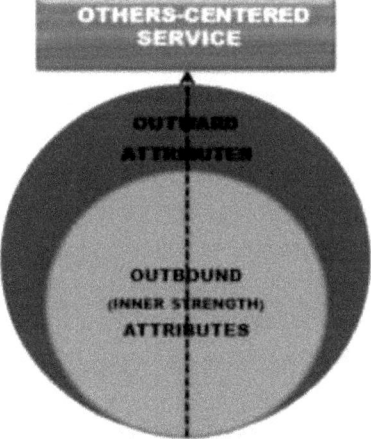

Figure 1.1. Servant leadership functional attributes

In summary, a leadership attribute is more than an ability or a characteristic; it is making those characteristics or abilities functional as part of how the leader acts (his habits) in service to others and applying those characteristics (beyond just having them) in personal and service relations to others. The character or known characteristic defines some aspects of your abilities or who you are inside— e.g. honest, humble, brave, etc. Your attribute, on the other hand, defines your habits; a display of how you use your characteristics, or the actions you exhibit toward others because of who you are inside. For example, empathy as a leadership characteristic becomes a leadership attribute if the followers can distinguish the leader's acts or habits of empathy, such as walking through with his followers in their state of suffering to bring wholeness; otherwise, it is just a characteristic or ability. Leadership attributes toward others are what impact the followers' and the organizational growth more than ability and competence.

In addressing one of the self-righteous hypocritical attributes of servitude leadership, Jesus called leader-servants to be "inside-out" leaders that reflect credibility; indeed, leaders should not appear outwardly righteous when they are full of hypocrisy and lawlessness in their hearts. He was describing "inside–out" as an authentic leadership attribute measured by the display of credibility a leadership attribute!

The measuring stick of a leader-servant is Jesus Christ. We measure ourselves unto the measure of the status of the fullness of Christ (Ephesians 4:13).

The leadership attributes of an authentic leader as a servant are encapsulated in **SERVANT/SERVING LEADERSHIP** are listed in Table 1.1, and defined in Table 1.2: *Servanthood, Emulation, Responsibility, Vision, Navigation, Adaptability, Trust, Listening, Empathy, Affection, Discipleship, Encouragement, Reproduction, Stewardship, Healing-Care, Initiation, Integrity,* and *Persuasion*. Other support attributes include *Influence, Courage, and Generosity*.

The attributes have been separated into Outward and Outbound (Inner Strength) leadership Attributes. As shown in Table 1.1, each of these attributes has three or more leadership characteristics. As such, more than 65 leadership characteristics are covered in these 20 attributes. For example, a leader's Servanthood leadership attribute is characterized by his willing servant's heart of selfless role humility, sacrifice, and submissiveness. The more these are present in a leader, the more effective the servant leadership.

Table 1.1: The functional leader-servant leadership Outbound (Inner Strength) and Outward attributes

	LEADER-SERVANT LEADERSHIP ATTRIBUTES			INNER STRENGTH ATTRIBUTES	OUTWARD ATTRIBUTES
S	Servanthood	L	Listening	Adaptability	Affection
E	Emulation	E	Empathy	Courage	Discipleship
R	Responsibility	A	Affection	Empathy	Emulation
V	Vision	D	Discipleship	Encouragement	Generosity
A	Adaptability	E	Encouragement	Initiation	Healing-Care
N	Navigation	R	Reproduction	Listening	Influence
T	Trust	S	Stewardship	Navigation	Persuasion
I	Influence	H	Healing-Care	Responsibility	Reproduction
G	Generosity	I	Initiation	Stewardship	Servanthood
C	Courage	P	Persuasion	Vision	Trust/Integrity

The list does not assume that a leader has to be excellent in all attributes or even have all of them to be an effective Leader–Servant. However, the more of these attributes the leader displays in his acts of service toward others, the more productive he or she will be, and the further his impact on the followers and organization. The table also shows that two or more attributes can share common characteristics, which can be applied or observed in different contexts. For example, a leader's ability to inspire followers can be seen in his acts of discipleship, empowerment, an.d encouragement attributes in the context in which these attributes apply. Each attribute is exhibited either as a part of the outbound inner strength attribute of a leader or a part of the outward attribute. Table 1.1 is not an exhaustive list of attributes; in fact, there are hundreds of such attributes. This is just the starting point.

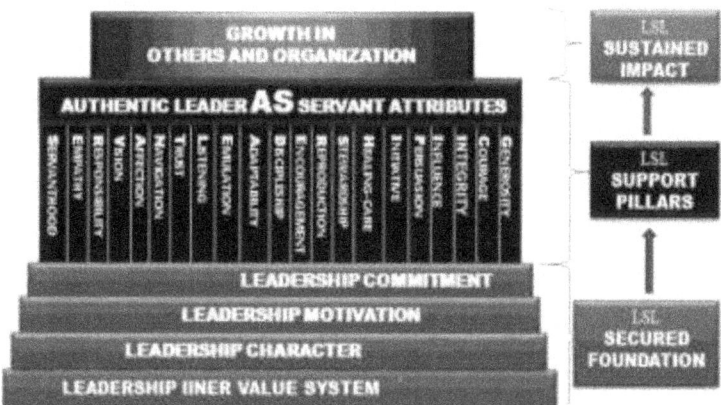

Figure 1.2: Servant leadership outward attributes (dark blue) and relationship to four foundational layers of the LSL Model

Figure 1.2 shows that the leader's attributes are shaped and secured by his four foundational layers (leadership inner value system, leadership character, motivation, and commitment). The attributes of the leader–servants are also conceptualized as the support pillars that will establish and support the personal authenticity of the leader, what the leader, does and the effectiveness of the leadership process. Thus, the attributes represent functional pillars of authentic leadership that can be learned or enriched as described in detail in the subsequent chapters. The combined effect of a secured foundation and stable support pillars will make a sustained impact on the growth of followers and the organization.

COMPARISONS WITH OTHER WORKS

The original works by Greenleaf (1970) in servant leadership [1] have been reviewed by Larry Spears (1996), who identified listening, empathy, healing, awareness, persuasion, conceptualization, foresight, stewardship, commitment to the growth of others, and building community as the ten distinguishing characteristics of servant leadership. [2] Russell (2001) has studied these attributes and have shown them to be essential in servant leadership and concluded that these qualities generally "grow out of the inner values and beliefs of individual leaders." [3] Russell and Stone (2002) extended the Greenleaf 10 attributes to 20 attributes observed in servant-leaders. These 20 attributes were categorized by these authors as either functional attributes (intrinsic characteristics of servant-leaders) or accompanying attributes (complement attributes that enhance the functional attributes).[4] The operational attributes were identified as vision, honesty, integrity, trust, modeling, service, pioneering, appreciation, and empowerment with the accompanying attributes of communication, credibility, competence, stewardship, visibility, influence, persuasion, listening, encouragement, teaching, and delegation. Only three of the attributes identified by Greenleaf were identified, and all three were accompanying attributes rather than functional. Responsibility, adaptability, affection, discipleship, navigation, and reproduction attributes which are considered critical in biblical-based servant leadership in my LSL model are not covered by Russell and Greenleaf. As shown in the description of the attributes in Table 1.2, most of the attributes reported by Russell and Stone (2002)[5] or Greenleaf [1] can be seen either in the twenty attributes or their associated characteristics. Integrity and honesty for example are leadership characteristics of trust and other attributes rather than an independent attributes. I take the position that servant leadership attributes are functional attributes in acts of duty to others and emanate from the inner value system of the leader.

CHAPTER 1
UNDERSTANDING LEADERSHIP ATTRIBUTES

Table 1.2: Description of the functional leader-servant outward leadership attributes and associated principles and charactcristics

Leader–Servant Leadership Attributes	Principles of Leadership Attributes	Leadership Characteristics
Affection: This is the combined love-based works toward providing the essential help or services for the spiritual growth or survival of another person. . (Chapter 2)	*Affection flows from a person to produce positive emotions for the well-being of another person*	Kindness Compassion Practical Love Affective signs Appreciation
Discipleship: This is the combined acts of personally developing, intentionally equipping, and attentively empowering growth in others to reproduce a heart of service. (Chapter 3)	*Discipleship transforms and empowers followers for service leadership that grows communities.*	Inspiring Shepherding Equipping Developing Empowering
Emulation: This is the combined acts of initiating an authentic servant attitude as a model of service worthy of following (Chapter 4)	*A great leader-servant outwardly and positively inspires a pattern of good works for others to follow.*	Inspiration Motivation Initiation Model Following
Generosity: This is the combined acts of freely sharing with and giving to others as an act of kindness, without expectation of reward or return to him. (Chapter 5)	*Generosity is an outward measure of the level of sacrifice, what is shared, or the impact a giving makes, not just the size of the giving.*	Sharing Giving Kindness Affection Love
Healing-Care: This is the combined acts of providing comfort and empathy to make others whole emotionally and spiritually along with tending to the follower's physical and mental well-being. (Chapter 6)	*Comforting others in any trouble with the comfort with which we are comforted by God, brings healing - wholeness.*	Self- Healing Empathy Reconciliation Comfort Relational
Influence: This is the combined acts of positively affecting desired change in conduct,	*The true measure of leadership success in affecting*	Model Positive attitude Authority

performance, and relational connections toward others-centered course of action or service. (Chapter 7)	*desired change in conduct, performance, and relational connections in others is influence*	Connection Wisdom Intelligence,
Persuasion: *This is the combined acts of communicating perspective to connect, challenge, and convince with a compelling purpose to convert others to a new position.* (Chapter 8)	*The means of transforming others to a new perspective is through empathetic persuasion*	Connecting Challenging Communicating Convincing Converting Encouraging
Reproduction: *This is the combined acts of developing your leadership qualities in others and releasing them as successors to continue a greater mission.* (Chapter 9)	*Great leaders produce successors for legacy and greater courses as an expected product of an effective leadership reproduction.*	Selecting Mentoring Equipping Empowering Releasing
Servanthood: *This is the combined acts of humility, willingness, and intentionality in service to others through selfless sacrifice and submission as a servant.* (Chapter 10)	*A leader-servant is most qualified to lead when most ready to serve as a servant for the growth of others. The role of a leader is to serve as a servant*	Servant's heart Humility Sacrifice Service Willingness Submissiveness
Trust: *This is the combined acts of positive display of character, competence, credibility, and shared relational connections that produce assured trust-confidence of the trustee in the trusted.* (Chapter 11)	*True leadership trust produces assured trustee's confidence and readiness to follow based on the credibility, competence, and shared relational connections of the trusted.*	Character Competence Integrity Credibility Confidence

PRINCIPLE OF LEADERSHIP ATTRIBUTE

In the context of servant leadership, a leadership attribute is a level above the leadership characteristic or trait of a leader. The principle of leadership attribute states that every leadership attribute has a set of distinguishing characteristics that make up the inward or outward display of the attribute. The principle reflects the essential designed purpose or outcome of the attribute or the inevitable consequence of the effective practice of the attribute. Thus, the principle of leadership attribute is a concise statement about the fundamental truth, value, or belief about the attribute in a leadership situation; it is a statement that establishes an idea about the outcome of the attribute for guiding the practical application of the attribute and its characteristics. I will postulate and frame each principle as an additive function of the characteristics of the attribute. A statement of each principle is quoted at the beginning or below the title of each chapter. It is yet to be experimentally proven if the attribute is a linear or some other non-linear function of these characteristics as variables. It is expected, however, that each character will contribute to the effectiveness of the attribute in varying degrees.

AUTHENTIC LEADERSHIP ATTRIBUTES

At a personal level, attributes are the value-based inside-out moral leadership assets that can be related to the authenticity of a leader-servant. The complexity of defining authenticity has been noted in the literature. The subject of authentic leadership is well covered in the works of Terry (1993),[5] George (2003),[6] and Shair and Eilam (2005).[7] All appear to agree that authenticity requires self-awareness and objective self-identity in personal and social interactions with others. In his book, *Advocacy Leadership*, Professor Gary L. Anderson offers individual, organizational, and societal perspectives on authenticity: "Authenticity, at a peculiar level, is living a life, whether in the private or professional term. This is congruent with one's espoused values; at the structural level, authenticity has to do with viewing human beings as ends in themselves, rather than means to other ends; at the public level, it is a state of affairs that is congruous with the shared political and cultural values of society."[8]

The basic tenets of these perspectives are very fitting to authenticity as a qualifying element of leader-servant leadership attributes. The attribute reflects how the followers see the leader based on the leader's distinctive features displayed through his or her actions personally, organizationally, and societally. The leader is seen as a leader-servant or serving leader because the followers see him lead as a servant from an inside-out value of others. This is what makes the leader authentic. Authenticity means that what a leader displays outside, in personal or leadership life of service to others, and society is based on the values the leader espouses inside.

Authenticity in servant leadership can be one or two types or both: *Outbound Authenticity and Outward Authenticity*. The Outbound (outward-bound) Authenticity is the genuineness of personal honesty from your inner strength and abilities; what you say and how you act emanate from who you are or how you feel inside. It reflects the essential truth and honesty about your outward-bound inner strength.

Outward authenticity, on the other hand, describes the truthfulness of your credibility and honesty displayed outward in relation to others; your *outer* visible behavior or how you act outwardly towards others reflects exactly your true intentions.

While *outward* authenticity is the visible *outer* indicator of the truth of who you are inside, *outbound* authenticity is outward-bound attribute from the inside of who you are. Credibility in this context is the influence a leader has to attract believability, trustworthiness, and authenticity; it is the believability, trustworthiness, and authenticity of who you are inside and outside.

A key element of personal authenticity is that it is seen or measured in the context of societal, cultural, and organizational interactions. In that context, achieving individual authenticity becomes a challenge since it is influenced by social factors and dispositions of individuals who usually depend on liberal and organizational realities. However, for leader-servant leadership, the leader can face those changing times by remaining focused on his key Biblical-based principles or *Leadership Inner Value System*. Thus, I am interested in authenticity as an essential element of effective Leader-servant leadership attributes or Leader-servant leadership attributes as drivers of leadership authenticity. With that in mind, the first critical element of authenticity in practicing or developing efficient leader-servant leadership attributes is inside-out self-examination relative to the people served rather than the organization. You may ask yourself: What will be my response when the people I lead act or react in a certain way, will it be negative or positive? What are my strengths and vulnerabilities at those times?

Professor Yacobi in his post, "Elements of Human Authenticity," noted that since "the self -arise attribute emerges from interactions between self, others, and the environment in a complex society and world, there may co-exist multiple complicated identities depending on place and context." [9] He went on to identify the following <u>essential elements of personal authenticity</u>: self-awareness, unbiased self-examination, accurate self-knowledge, reflective judgment, personal responsibility, and integrity, genuineness, and humility, empathy for others, understanding of others, optimal utilization of feedback from others. All of these are covered under the leadership attributes or characteristics shown in Table 1.2.

Bill George, in his book, *Authentic Leadership*, takes the position that to be an authentic leader; a person must have the following essential characteristics: [10]

- Behavior based on value: He must understand his own values and exhibit behavior to others based on those values;
- He must not compromise his values in difficult situations but could use the situation to strengthen personal values in those situations.
- Passion from a clear purpose: Be self-aware of who he is, where he is going, and the right thing to do.
- Compassion from the heart: He must lead from a compassionate heart that allows them to be sensitive to the plight and needs of others,
- Connectedness from a relationship; he must be relationally connected with people he leads,
- Consistency from the self-disciple: He must demonstrate self-discipline to remain calm, collected, and consistent in a stressful situation.

Modeled after the elements above, Table 1.3 lists six essential characteristics of authenticity for servant leadership. These fundamental characteristics cover the five identified above and can also be aligned with the leadership characteristics in Table 1.2. Each attribute in Table 1.2 is expected to pass the personal authenticity test in Tables 1.3, 1.4. In a survey of 132 Christian leaders, seventy-four percent (74%) of them agreed that they always or frequently exhibit servant leadership attributes.[11] Thus, a pass of the outward authenticity test means that a pure leader must demonstrate 70% or more of these essential elements of this legitimacy. (That is, 70% YES in the assessment questions in Tables 1.3, 1.4).

It needs to be noted, however, that a secular leader could be authentic and still lack some of the essential servant leadership attributes or characteristics such as selflessness, servanthood, and love-motivated servant attitudes of a leader-servant. Effective leader-servants are authentic leaders and personal authenticity is an essential element of leader-servant leadership. The key test for leader-servant authenticity is the quality of his inside-out value and personal character. What is most important is a change from the inside-out.

Table 1.3: The test of essential elements of personal inner strength authenticity in servant leadership			
	Elements of Inner Strength Authenticity	Inner Strength (Outbound) Authenticity Assessment Questions	YES / NO
1	Personal inside-out value-based behavior	Are your personal inside-out values aligned with acts of service and behavior outside?	1
		Are you honest to yourself in relation to your inner strengths and abilities?	2
2	Inside-out Self-Awareness	Do you have unbiased self-examination, and accurate self-knowledge of who you are inside-out?	3
		Do you know your inner strength and weaknesses in relation to the good you want to show as an outward attribute?	4
3	Inside-out Empathy-Compassion	Do you know and feel from your inside what you want for your followers?	5
		Are you motivated to empathize, based on your inside feelings?	6
4	Inside-out Connection with followers	Do you feel deep, personal, and spiritual connection with your followers?	7
		Does what you say and how you act reflect how you feel when you relate to others?	8
5	Inside-out Emotional Self-regulation	Do you have difficulty controlling your emotion in order to remain calm in a stressful situation?	9
		Are you always able to comfort yourself?	10
6	Inside-out Authenticity Feedback	Do your followers see your inside-out value from your outside behavior?	11
		Will your followers feel that what you say you are is congruent with how you act?	12
#YESs_____ ; # NOs_____ : Outbound Authenticity: YES/ 12————%			

Table 1.4: The test of essential elements of personal outward authenticity in servant leadership

	Elements of Personal Outward Authenticity	Personal Outward Authenticity Assessment Questions	YES or NO
1	Personal value-based outward behavior	Are your personal values and beliefs aligned with your acts of service and behavior toward others?	1
		Do you live out your life according to your beliefs?	2
2	Personal Self-Awareness	Do you have clarity of your personal vision and purpose?	3
		Does what you know about yourself accurately describe what others say?	4
3	Personal Outward Empathy-Compassion	Do you apply how you feel to what your followers need?	5
		Do you lead from a compassionate heart and are you sensitive to the plight and needs of others?	6
4	Personal Connection with followers	Do you feel deep, personal connection with your followers?	7
		Does your outward action toward others reflect exactly your true intentions?	8
5	Outward Emotional Self-regulation	Do you have difficulty controlling your emotions to remain calm in a stressful situation?	9
		Does your evaluation of your value of others agree with how valued they feel?	10
6	Personal Authenticity Feedback	Do your followers see your outward acts as true and honest?	11
		Can your followers see other-centeredness in 70% or more of your attributes?	12

#YESs_____; # NOs_____; Outward Authenticity: YES/ 12 ———————%

ALS Healing-Care Leadership Attributes, Principles, & Practices

Table 1.5. Leader As Servant-Leadership Audit							
A servant-leader in his leadership position purposefully choses to serve and inspire acts of service in others by his example. Select and circle best answer to questions 1=Never: 2=Almost never ; 3=Sometimes; 4=Frequently; 5 =Always							
	Servant Leadership assessment questions	Circle no				
1	I am willing and other-centered, and readily chose to serve others as a servant for their personal growth	1	2	3	4	5
2	I model others-centered attitude in my service and relationships and inspire same for others to follow	1	2	3	4	5
3	I have a sense of obligation, willingness, and accountability for the service towards others	1	2	3	4	5
4	I have the foresightedness to specify in the present view what others' growth should be in a given future	1	2	3	4	5
5	I work toward providing the essential help or services for the spiritual growth or survival of the others;	1	2	3	4	5
6	I provide the needed purposeful course of action for how to chart the course to for my followers.	1	2	3	4	5
7	I display external credibility and a strong sense of character based on values, beliefs, and competence;	1	2	3	4	5
8	In communication, I attentively perceive and hear what is communicated, reflectively listen to understand and to be understood	1	2	3	4	5
9	I walk through with others in their state (suffering, emotions, etc.) in a way that provides the needed care and well-being	1	2	3	4	5
10	I have a measure of self-secured flexibility to adapt appropriate attitude to serve all people in different situations	1	2	3	4	5
11	I personally develop, intentionally equip, and attentively nurture spiritually growth in others	1	2	3	4	5
12	My act of bravery instills in others the courage and confidence to follow or persevere in a course of action	1	2		4	5
13	I develop my leadership qualities in others as successors to continue in a purposeful mission	1	2	3	4	5
14	I manage , maintain,, and account for all resources entrusted to me and being responsible for the difference my acts make	1	2	3	4	5
15	As a care-giver, I act to comfort and make others whole emotionally	1	2	3	4	5
16	When I see a need, I originate a vision and action, and stay committed to meet that need and desired change	1	2	3	4	5

17	I display a holistic view of an issue to inform, transform or convert others to my view through empathetic persuasion	1	2	3	4	5
18	I freely share what I have sacrificially as an act of kindness to others, without expectation of reward in return	1	2	3	4	5
19	My act of influence is to affect the actions, behavior, opinions, etc., of others based on trust, credibility and relationship	1	2	3	4	5
20	In the face challenges and danger, I act with bravery to overcome fear and take a stand with strength and conviction	1	2	3	4	5
Score Range	Add up the numbers in each column (Total Score____ Check and Understand the key areas to work on					
81-100	Strong Leader-Servant; keep it up, go and train others.					
66-80	Above average Leader-Servant; work 25% of key areas					
50-65	Average but developing; need to work on 50% of key areas					
34-49	Below average leader; work on 75% of key areas					
<34	Not a Leader-Servant; need training in all areas					

Summary 1
Understanding Leadership Process

Before starting this exercise, please read and follow the instruction in the preface of this workbook. Answers to these questions are contained in this chapter. Completion of these exercises after reading the chapter should take 60-90 minutes.

Discovering the Leadership Attributes

1. What is your alternative definition of leadership? In learning to lead, how would you differentiate the following elements:
    a. Leadership,
    b. Leader as servant leadership.
    c. Leadership characteristics.
    d. Leadership attributes
2. What are the key differences between the Leader as Servant and the Servant as Leader Leadership philosophies?
3. What was the original source of the Servant as Leader (SL)?

4. What is the key framework of a Leader as a Servant Leadership?
5. Authenticity in servant leadership can be one or two types or both *Outbound Authenticity and Outward Authenticity*: Describe a time when you displayed:
    a. The Outbound (outward-bound)— *outbound* authenticity is outward-bound attribute from the inside of who you are.
    b. *The Outward Authenticity*—*outward* authenticity is the visible *outer* indicator of the truth of who you are inside,
6. Describe the key elements of personal authenticity seen or measured in the context of societal, cultural, and organizational interactions.
7. How are the essential characteristics of authentic leader in leadership process in challenging times.
8. How much of a leader-servant are you? Take the personal leader-servant audit in Table 1.5.
9. Based on the questions in Table 1.5, can you identify each of the twenty attributes? What ones did you score 3 ("sometimes") or less than 3?

CHAPTER 2
LEADERSHIP HEALING-CARE ATTRIBUTE

Comforting others in any trouble with the comfort with which we are comforted by God, brings healing-wholeness

Effective leadership begins with an emotionally and spiritually healthy leader who can reconcile and bring comfort to the followers, irrespective of followers' feelings (good or bad) toward the leader. The healing attribute and personal security complement each other. You must have the capacity for self-healing and individual security if you are to meet others' comforts for several reasons. First, insecure leaders cause their organizations to plateau and people to be hurt. Personal security provides the infrastructure to support leaders in adversity and heal others that are hurting. Second, insecure leaders can hardly empower and develop secure followers. A leader's or a group's success is measured by the strength of the weakest member or follower. A leader-servant has the ability as a caregiver to comfort and make others whole emotionally and spiritually.

Healing is one of the most abstract and least understood attributes in this book, and yet in my estimation one of the most important. Why? Because it crosses over most of the other outward and outbound attributes-empathy, responsibility, accountability, etc. Many years ago, my two children, Emi and her brother HeCareth had a motor accident that changed the life of my daughter Emi. Her brother was driving her back to her campus in Johnstown in January, which is known to be one of the most dangerous months to drive to Summerset, Pennsylvania. The road was so bad that people were advised to stay home unless they had to travel. Well, Emi had good reason to go because she had exams and projects to complete. Four miles before the Summerset exit leading to Johnson, their car skidded uncontrollably off the road, went off a cliff, and plunged 150 feet below, a few feet from the Alleghany River at the bottom. Some trees prevented the car from plunging into the river. Fortunately, an 18-wheeler truck driver who observed them driving down stopped and called the police. For 45 minutes, however, my children were at the bottom of the valley where they landed. They managed to emerge from the car but were faced with two feet of snow. Emi had lost her shoes and had to stand on her brother's toes for warmth. He was hurt more badly than she was, but he still took extra steps to see that his frightened sister was as well and tried to keep her awake. He was showing Healing Care! She was in danger of falling into a coma. Before the police and ambulance arrived, they were almost frozen to death. They came out alive with only minor bruises. According to police they were not supposed to survive that accident. A similar accident happened the year before that was not as severe, and all four people in the car died. In response, Emi said, "Daddy, God gave me a second chance to live again." Unfortunately, for years after the accident, Emi was afraid of driving.

In the aftermath of the 11 September 2001 tragedy, what was needed the most was communal healing for the families who lost loved ones, which was care and compassion. The collective response occurs when organized action is taken to foster healing or restoration. According to Kanov et al (2004), [23] compassion can be enabled through three processes: cooperative noticing, united feeling, and concerted responding. Communal noticing occurs when people during a difficult time such as the September 11 incident or mass shooting in a school, become aware of the incident and volunteer to seek out others that need help. Such actions usually bring the community together out of a common desire to express compassion. The community coming jointly results in the next level of combined feeling where people collectively express and share their feelings and emotions through planned public events. Based on those meetings, the act of compassion can move to the level of collective responding, such as writing letters to the government, lobbying for change in laws, or peaceful demonstrations. All these three levels work together to foster a climate of compassion.

CHAPTER 2
LEADERSHIP HEALING-CARE ATTRIBUTE

What is healing-Care and what does it mean in practical terms to you as a leader? What does the Bible say about bodily healing and health? Answers to these and other related questions are explored in this chapter. Again, we will identify the key distinguishing characteristics and formulate a working definition and principle of leadership healing-care attributes based on those characteristics. Each characteristic will be discussed in detail with emphasis on strategies of how they can be further developed or practiced by a leader-servant as part of the servant leadership process.

PRINCIPLE OF HEALING-CARE ATTRIBUTE

We can surmise, based on the above discussions, that a leader's leadership healing-care attribute to bring wholeness to others can be characterized by his acts of *Self-Healing, Empathy, Reconciliation, and Comfort* of others and himself, leading us to a working definition:

The Servant-Leadership Healing Care Attribute is the combined acts of providing comfort and empathy to make others whole emotionally and spiritually along with tending to the follower's physical and psychological well-being.

Healing the wholeness of someone includes the act of filling gaps in the person's emotional, spiritual, physical, and mental wholeness to the human extent possible and recognizing that it is God that ultimately brings lasting cures and wholeness. The primary outcome of Healing-Care Attribute is the wholeness and well-being of another person. This can be stated as follows:

Servant leadership Healing Care Principle: Comforting others in any trouble with the consolation with which we are relieved by God brings healing - wholeness.

This outcome of this attribute can be expressed as a four-dimensional, linearly dependent cause-and-effect relationship on our wholeness as:

$$\text{SELF-HEALING} + \text{EMPATHY} \\ + \text{RECONCILIATION} + \text{COMFORT} \\ = \text{WHOLENESS HEALING - CARE}$$

Figure 6 shows the inter-relationship between the characteristics of leadership healing Care (Self-Healing, Empathy, Reconciliation, and Comfort) and the four states of well-being (spiritual, emotional, mental, and physical) of human wholeness.

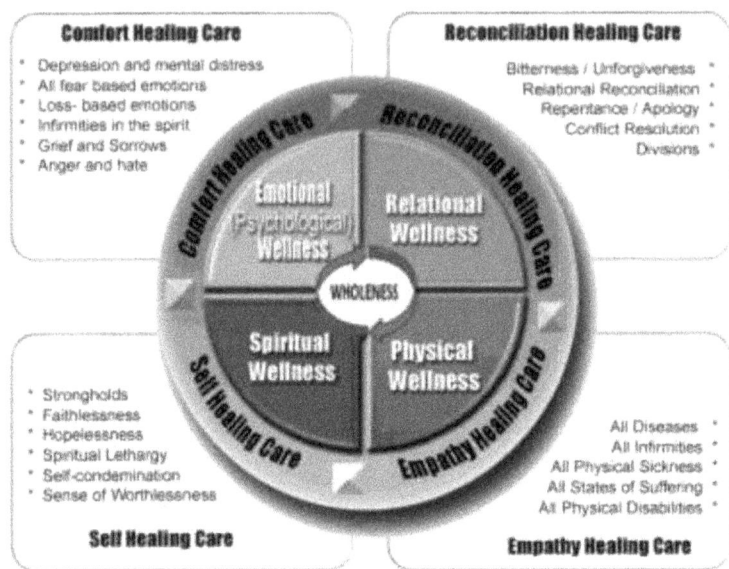

Figure 6: Inter-relationship model of four states of the well-being of human servant leadership healing-care attribute

Can a leader-servant heal or help his or her followers develop wholeness? The answer is an absolute yes. One of the essences of servant leadership is to help others become whole through service.

SUMMARY 2
LEADERSHIP HEALING-CARE ATTRIBUTE

Before starting this exercise, please read and follow the instruction in the preface of this workbook. Answers to these questions are contained in this chapter. Completion of these exercises after reading the chapter should take 60-90 minutes.

Discovering Healing-Care Leadership Attribute

1. What is healing Care and why is it an important leadership attribute?

Chapter 2
Leadership Healing-Care Attribute

2. What is healing Care and what does it mean in practical terms to you as a leader?
3. What does the Bible say about bodily healing and health?
4. What are the distinguishing characteristics of leadership healing-care?
5. Define *Servant-Leadership Healing Care Attribute in the context of its characteristics*
6. What is the primary outcome of Healing-Care Attribute is the wholeness and well-being of another person?
7. State the *Servant leadership Healing Care Principle*
8. State the additive law of law of Healing-Care Leadership attribute
9. How can a leader-servant heal or help his or her followers develop wholeness?

Practicing Healing Care- Attribute

1. What would you consider the key characteristics of healing care leadership attributes?
2. How many acts of healing care as an attribute do you display?
3. Take the Leadership Healing care attribute audit in Table 6

Table 12.6. Leadership Healing-Care Attribute Audit

Servant leadership healing care attribute is the combined acts of providing comfort and empathy to make others whole emotionally and spiritually Assess the quality of your acts of healing care attribute by inserting an X below the number that best describes your response to each statement.

Item	Acts of Healing Care Attribute Check 1= Always; 2= Frequently; 3= Sometimes; 4= Almost Never; 5= Never	1	2	3	4	5
1	I have the emotional and spiritual capacity to comfort myself and others					
2	I act in ways to build up and support the wholeness of others					
3	I Invite the presence of God into the healing process through fervent prayers.					
4	I develop a sense of oneness and obligation to meet the healing-wholeness of others					
5	I comfort my followers and assure them of their self-worth					
6	I walk through with others in their own state of suffering.					
7	I provide comfort and empathy to make others whole emotionally and spiritually					
8	My sense of personal healing affect my inner strength to face challenges competently and to help others,					
9	I continuously gauge my action and their impact on others					
10	My self-healing or wholeness of others begins with total forgiveness and reconciliation					
	Add up your rating in each column					
Score Range	Guide and Explanation of Score: understand the areas you need to further develop			Score		
10-17	Great Healing care leadership; keep it up!					
18-25	Above Average Healing Care; need to work on 25% of the areas					
26-33	Average for greatness; need to work on 50% of the areas					
34-41	Below average- healing care, need to work on 75% of the areas					
42-50	No healing care leadership ; work in all the areas					

CHAPTER 3
DEVELOPING WHOLENESS – SELF-HEALING

Self-healing is the emotional and inner capacity of the leader to comfort him- or herself with the comfort he or she receives from God and how he extends the same healing to others. Your state of spiritual well-being could be due to things such as a lack of forgiveness, a need for reconciliation with someone, a state of hopelessness, infirmities in the spirit or diseases in the body, or struggles with works of the flesh. Whatever they might be; a leader must be healed of them. Your follower may also be going through the same low state of spiritual well-being. You must first heal yourself to be strong enough to heal others.

He must hold on to God's promises of protection from diseases by diligently walking with God and hearing from God. In developing the personal self-healing that enables him or her to heal others, the leader-servant needs to invite the presence of God, develop a sense of oneness with the followers, a sense of self-worth, a sense of purpose, and self-efficacy in his own healing in relation to others' healing. Here are some examples of how we can develop in these five areas:

CHARACTERISTICS OF HEALING-CARE ATTRIBUTE

God desires not only for us to prosper in good health and sound mind, but also to desire wholeness for humanity. This is equally important that is required from the leader-servant; that is, the desire to see wholeness in all of his or her followers. This includes commitment and working with God to ensure that the followers are cared for. John desired that his followers be whole. He assured them when he said; "Beloved, I pray that you may prosper in all things and be in health, just as your soul prospers." 3 John 1:2

Wholeness has four critical elements: physical, relational, emotional/ psychological, and spiritual healing that make us complete.

All these elements are additive and intertwined in the bodily and mental wholeness of humans. This means that issues with one element can cause issues with another. Because the mind, body, soul, and spirit are entirely connected, emotional trauma such as anger, sadness, and depression can be linked to physical illness. In most cases, human emotion is a response to an experience, or imagined situation in the past, present, or future. For example, a breakdown in a relationship between loved ones can affect emotional wellness; the memory of a serious car accident experienced in the past in which someone died can create an emotional fear of driving in the present. The life that was spared in that same accident can also increase our faith (spiritual wellness) and love for God.

Basic human emotions can be traced to some degree during heartfelt, love-based, fear-based, and spirit-based situations. Examples of loved-based emotions include such feelings as desire, pleasure, contentment, acceptance, peacefulness, excitement, patience, self-esteem, assertiveness, and generosity. Fear-based emotions include anxiety, contention, envy, anger, selfishness, sorrow, bitterness, jealousy, depression, irritability, rejection, and aggression. A few examples of spirit-based emotions include faith, love, hope, peace, faithfulness, gentleness, patience, and all fruits of the spirit (Galatians 5:22-23).

From the above introduction, we can deduce that wholeness healing care requires *emotional and spiritual* wellness along with healing *physical* diseases and the mental health of followers. All must be considered for absolute wholeness, even though a leader may not be professionally equipped or trained to handle all four dimensions. However, it is a part of *a caring* attitude to understand these dimensions and to provide recommendations for attention when needed. We know that our thoughts stir up our emotions, and our emotions and resulting feelings as responses influence our desires and ultimate behavior.

Our wholeness depends on our physical, mental, emotional (psychological), and spiritual states. Although sentimental behavior is a condition or feeling of the heart, if unchecked, the stress that results can affect a person mentally and physically. As noted, not all leaders work in the medical profession for physical healing, but all leaders can be used as part of God's plan for bringing absolute wholeness to the body of Christ or members of an organization. The contribution of each of these elements to wholeness may not be equal. For example, a person's

Chapter 3
Developing Wholeness–Self-Healing

ailments may be more than 30% due to emotional issues, compared to 40% spiritual, and the remaining 30% due to physical and mental states. Understanding where we are in each of these states of wholeness is the beginning of self-healing or healing with the assistance of a leader-servant.

An important aspect of a leader's ability to bring wholeness to others falls in the effectiveness of his or her ministry of reconciliation and comfort. Emotional sickness can be the result of hurt caused by a lack of forgiveness or conflicts between two or more people in a fellowship.

This is sometimes seen in churches among believers, between husband and wife, and between relatives. However, we also see leaders who have problems forgiving their followers for offenses or lack the empathy to comfort those who are hurting. Such leaders lose credibility in trying to reconcile differences between followers.

Paul addressed this issue and reminded us that it is God "Who has reconciled us to Himself through Jesus Christ, and has given us the ministry of reconciliation"

(2 Corinthians 5:18). The healing attribute of the Leader-Servant is a measure of his potential to treat himself and others of hurts and disappointments and allows him or her to recognize opportunities to help make whole followers with whom he comes in contact. His comfort allows him to comfort others in his ministry of reconciliation. Reconciliation must be the goal in the healing attribute through the strength of comfort we receive from God. Paul wrote, "For the Father of mercies and God of all comfort, who comforts us in all our tribulations, that we may be able to comfort those who are in any trouble, with the comfort with which we ourselves are comforted by God" (2 Corinthians 1:2-4).

INVITING GOD INTO THE HEALING PROCESS

Inviting the presence of God into the healing process occurs through fervent prayers. The power of a leader-servant's prayer with his trusted inner circle over his situation or that of a hurting member can go very far. Healing miracles can be activated through such fervent prayers or sometimes fasting over situations. Leaders are commanded to do this; "Is anyone among you sick? Let him call for the elders of the church, and let them pray over him, anointing him with oil in the name of the Lord." James 5:14 The power and effectiveness of such a ministry by a leader depend on his own wholeness and ability to put others' needs above his particular need. Jesus' purpose in healing others was to cleanse the entire fellowship of their suffering and deliver them from pain, even at the cross when he forgave one of the criminals who was hung beside him (Luke 23:39-42). A leader must also invite those he trusts or to whom he feels accountable to pray for or with him.

Developing a Sense of Oneness

The body of Christ is one, and the health of the group is often measured by the spiritual health and vision of the leader. If a leader has a sense of meeting the healing-wholeness obligation to his followers, he must work on his own wholeness through the comfort that comes from God. Leader-servants must recognize that their primary responsibility is to help make whole those with whom they come into contact as one healthy body of Christ. It is the hands of the leader the Chief Healer will use to bring healing in some cases. Our capacity to walk through the valley of that physical or emotional situation is as powerful as the medication human doctors prescribe. It may even be the only medication needed. The leader must lead the followers to recognize that members of the organization are perfectly joined together in the same mind.

Developing a sense of Self-worth in Healing

Part of healing wholeness for others is comforting them and assuring them of their self-worth to God. God loved us so much that Christ died for us, even in our worthless state. To be effective in communicating this message, the leader must display a strong inner self and sense of worth. In my life, I have had friends who acknowledged that they received significant emotional strength and comfort that God can meet our everyday needs by watching me display my faith and self-worth in God. This demonstrates that your words of encouragement and comfort go a long way to uplift someone else when you live those words.

DEVELOPING A SENSE OF PURPOSE IN HEALING

A sense of purpose is a feeling that you are not only important to God but also your followers depend on you for their wholeness. It is a feeling that God created you for a purpose that only you, walking with Him, can fulfill. Hence, you must work on your healing by self-regulating areas of your life that can take you away from the purpose of serving others. As a leader-servant, healing others is an important act of service in your ministry. This means that you must walk with God for your healing if you must meet the obligation of healing others.

DEVELOPING SELF-EFFICACY FOR THE HEALING

How can a leader bring healing to others, unless he has a feeling that God can use Him as a vehicle for that purpose? Self-healing often depends on one's sense of self-security, self-leadership, and self-efficacy. A leader's values affect his self-efficacy and his belief in his power and competence through faith to produce the desired outcome of healing others. This has been true in my life. Every time I needed personal healing, a strong sense of self-efficacy, borne out of full faith and experience with God, has positively activated my spiritual power to face challenges competently, but the choices I made in such given situations.

SUMMARY 3
DEVELOPING WHOLENESS–SELF-HEALING

Before starting this exercise, please read and follow the instruction in the preface of this workbook. Answers to these questions are contained in this chapter. Completion of these exercises after reading the chapter should take 60-90 minutes.

Discovering Wholeness Self-healing

1. What is self-healing?
2. What does the scripture teach about self-sealing (3 John 1:2)
3. What are the distinguishing characteristics of Healing-Care Attribute
4. Basic human emotions can be traced to some degree during heartfelt, love-based, fear-based, and spirit-based situations. Give some examples of each (Galatians 5:22-23).
5. Our wholeness depends on our physical, mental, emotional (psychological), and spiritual states. Why are all four contribution of each of these elements to wholeness
6. How does the healing attribute help make to make followers whole (2 Corinthians 1:2-4).

Practicing Healing-Care Attribute

1. Self-Healing is the emotional and spiritual capacity of a leader to comfort himself with the comfort he/she receives from God and his extension of the same healing to others.
2. How can a leader develop in these five areas?
   a. Sense of Oneness with your Followers
   b. Sense of self-efficacy for your healing
   c. Sense of self-security, self-leadership, and self-efficacy
   d. How you invite God into the healing process (James 5:14; Luke 23:39-42).
3. How can developing a Sense of Oneness bring healing
4. How can developing a Sense of Purpose bring about in Healing
5. In Developing self-efficacy for the Healing

CHAPTER 4
DEVELOPING THE ACTS OF HEALING-EMPATHY

Empathy Healing-Care is the act of responsiveness to walk with others through their own states of suffering. It means intentionally extending caregiving actions to assist in other's fleshy well-and emotional, Empathy Healing-Care is especially critical in all physical sicknesses, infirmities, and all states of suffering requiring the leader to walk through the bodily state and the associated emotions with the hurting person. Empathy healing-care giving actions could include the following:

IDENTIFY WITH STATE OF SUFFERING AND INFIRMITIES

What did Jesus bear in Isaiah 53:4-5? He bore our griefs, sorrows (pains), the feebleness of mind, frailties, sicknesses, weaknesses, infirmities, diseases, and so on. Infirmities are any physical weakness in body, soul, spirit, and ability; sicknesses are bodily diseases. Infirmities differ from diseases. One can have infirmities but not diseases. For example, Paul had infirmities because of his suffering but no indication of sickness and disease (2 Corinthians 11:24-30, 12:5-10; Galatians 4:13). Jesus bore the grief, sorrow, sicknesses, and afflictions of humanity; "by His stripes, we are healed" (Isaiah 53: 4-5). The leader-servant must bear the emotional and spiritual states of his or her followers by being intimately connected with their healing until they achieve wholeness. The ultimate leader-servant, Jesus, was stricken, wounded, bruised, chastised, and humiliated as evidenced by the stripes on his body. Eventually, He died as a ransom for the wholeness and abundant life of His followers. As Peter said; "Who Himself bore our sins in His own body on the tree, that we, having died to sins, might live for righteousness—by whose stripes you were healed" (1 Peter 2:24, NKJV).

Physically and emotionally connect to bring healing to others when possible.

How did Jesus go about healing people? Jesus physically touched the sick, in some cases in the areas where they were hurting; their ears, eyes, or hand. The sick and those who had fallen out of faith sought out and touched Jesus. "And as many as touched Him were made well" (Mark 6:56). Very often, leaders receive phone calls from a member of the fellowship or congregation for earnest support, especially during the loss of a loved one, marital difficulty, children issues (especially among single parents), loss of employment, and so on. Such phone calls are like reaching out and touching the leader for support and must be handled with all purposeful urgency such as a visit with elders in the fellowship, praying for emotional healing; lending open ears to listen to the hurt, and offering needed encouragement.

Take intentional actions that contribute to the wholeness

Jesus himself reminded us of this: "For I was hungry and you gave me something to eat, I was thirsty and you gave me something to drink, I was a stranger and you invited me in, I needed clothes and you clothed me, I was sick and you looked after me, I was in prison and you came to visit me" (Matthew 25:35-36, NIV). Jesus' statement was a surprise to the people. He made it clear that our service to each other or to any one of these that Jesus loves, and has come to die for, and that is all humanity, is a service to Him. He said, "…As you did it to one of least of one these my brethren you did it to me" (Matthew 25:40, NIV). As leader-servants, we may not die for our followers, because Jesus already paid the price once and for all, but we must be willing to lay down our pride and make all possible sacrifices for the wholeness of the followers. "Greater love has no one than this: to lay down one's life for one's friends" (John 15:13). This was so important to the Lord that He wanted to make sure that, deep down, Peter was committed to the healingcare of His lambs and sheep as shown in His last few words before He ascended to Heaven. Three times He asked Peter, "Do you love Me?" To Peter's three affirmative answers, Jesus responded, "feed My Lambs", "tend My sheep", or "feed My Sheep" (John 21:15-17, NKJV). Peter in his answer to the first question, "Do you love Me more than these", responded, "Yes, Lord; You know that

I love You" but omitted the reference to the real emphasis "more than these" (John 21:15) …putting the sincerity of his heart in question. Peter was grieved perhaps on the reflection for his denial of Christ; His faith and love were not in doubt as much as his conduct, courage, and resilience in challenging times. He needed full faith and courage for the responsibilities ahead. The Leader-servants are purely qualified to serve to feed the sheep and lambs of Christ only if they love Christ the good Shepherd more than any earthly materials, rights, or objects. Our actions must be conscious efforts to care for the followers—providing the needed spiritual and physical necessities whenever possible, and healing to touch the souls of the hurting and hungry world. Intentional actions that contribute to the wholeness of others include the following:

Continuously gauge your actions and their impact on followers. Continuously gauge your actions and their impact on followers. The healing attribute calls for ceaselessly gauging our actions and their impact on the people we serve. Leaders, when not careful, can cause emotional sickness in their followers. This can come in the form of disrespecting your followers, verbal abuse, being demeaning, and being condescending in your relationship, participating in gossip, and servitude leadership actions, all of which can cause heart-rending damage. The best way to heal is to prevent or avoid behaviors that cause the sickness in the first place.

Provide opportunities to release and transform negative emotions. Leaders, even if they are offended, must provide opportunities for the hurting to release and transform the negative emotion into positive action by working with the person and relating to their feelings. This helps the person take responsibility for self-healing.

Be an empathetic reflective Influencer. As fully discussed elsewhere, to be sensitive and guard against actions that do not contribute to wholeness, a leader must empathize with followers. The leader can do so by reflecting to understand the other person's experience and point of view by looking at issues from their perspective. They must also let go of preconceived ideas, have an open mind, empathize by reflecting on the content, and feel at a greater level to understand what may be deeper issues. The leader must understand the unspoken words by focusing on spiritual concerns (self-esteem, meaning, hopes, fears, etc.) to understand the issues, and listen to the emotions and feelings expressed: words in the spirit (emotions, hurts, joys, etc. hidden in words).

Look for affirmations. Emotional healing often requires simple affirmative words to build up a person, particularly because some issues may be low self-esteem. Use statements that will produce a favorable outlook in the mind of the hurting. Various tools of beneficial self-talk can be used to transform negative thinking patterns into increased positive feelings. This is also a place a leader can connect spiritually with the hurting person through shared beliefs, faith, and prayer to enhance awareness of God's presence in the healing process.

Expending yourself and energy to the things you can control. A leader can only pursue with 100% energy what he can attract and control. We can attract the best to us by first seeking God and doing what is most important to Him (Matthew 6:25-33). If you are uncertain about what the follower needs, it is always a good strategy to ask. For example, some people are very private. One could ask, "What you are experiencing is like what I went through when I was doing so things. Would you like me to share that experience with you?" In this way, you show authenticity in walking with the person through the experience.

SUMMARY 4
DEVELOPING THE ACTS OF HEALING-EMPATHY

Before starting this exercise, please read and follow the instruction in the preface of this workbook. Answers to these questions are contained in this chapter. Completion of these exercises after reading the chapter should take 60-90 minutes.

Discovering the Acts of Healing-Empathy

Healing-Empathy is the responsiveness to walk through with others in their own state of suffering.
1. How can healing-care empathy bring emotional or spiritual healing to others?
2. List some actions you take as a leader for Healing-empathy care-of your followers
3. Hw would you continuously gauge your actions and their impact on Followers?
4. What is empathy healing-care and why is it critical in all physical sicknesses and states of suffering?

CHAPTER 4
DEVELOPING THE ACTS OF HEALING-EMPATHY

5. How did Jesus demonstrate that taking intentional actions in followers suffering bring the wholeness of his followers?. (Matthew 25:35-36, NIV). (Matthew 25:40, NIV). (John 15:13). (John 21:15-17, NKJV).

Practicing Empathy-Healing Care

1. In identifying with the suffering of followers as a strategy for healing care, what did Jesus bear in
   (Isaiah 53:4-5?; 1 Peter 2:24, NKJV).
2. For leader Connecting Emotionally to Bring Healing, how did Jesus go about healing people? (Mark 6:56).
3. How do the following intentional actions contribute to the wholeness of others?:
    a. Continuously gauge your actions and their impact on followers.
    b. Provide opportunities to release and transform negative emotions.
    c. Be an empathetic reflective Influencer.
    d. Look for affirmative words to build up a person.
    e. Expending yourself and energy to the things you can control (Matthew 6:25-33)?

CHAPTER 5
DEVELOPING WHOLENESS-RECONCILIATION

Reconciliation wholeness healing-care attitude is the specific action taken to resolve conflicts to bring healing to a broken relationship between the leader and others or between followers. As a leader, has somebody ever lied against you, betrayed your trust, cheated you, cheated on you, enslaved you, abused you, stolen from you, or physically or emotionally hurt you? Or have you done any of these to any of your followers or on any account lacked forgiveness or had a grudge against someone? One of the practical lessons we learned from the Calvary cross was that Jesus commanded us to forgive those that hurt us. The hurt can come in different forms. A hurt occurs when someone or something causes a detriment or damage to your health or feelings. In general, it hurts to make us physically, mentally, spiritually, and emotionally sick. When Jesus was flogged, humiliated, and nailed to the cross and "was bruised for our iniquities…" (Isaiah 53:5, NKJV) he was hurt. Nevertheless, he said, "Father forgive them, they do not know what they do…" (Luke 23:34).

Pastor Lance Lecocq of Monroeville Assembly of God defined reconciliation as a situation "when enemies become friends." Additionally, wholeness–reconciliation is an act of harmonizing relationships and developing mutual respect between enemies to make them whole emotionally and relationally. Reconciliation occurs between family members, lovers, friends, organizations, and despite of businesses, not just enemies, because conflicts are expected to arise even in the best of relationships, including marriages between two Christians. Reconciliation provides healing time, the opportunity to make amends in relationships, a time of forgiveness, acceptance, understanding, and whole healing of hurts. Humans are not wired to remain in a state of anger and hurtful feelings for too long without serious health consequences. To be mentally healthy, humans must control their feelings and not allow hurts from conflicting experiences to negatively rule their lives. Research shows that sustained emotional instability from things such as anger can increase blood pressure, cause headaches, and cause anxiety that may cause physical health problems such as ulcers or heart disease. Often, it is the person that needs to forgive—the offender—not the offended, that ends up hurting themselves the most and blocking the blessings of God from their lives. The following principles can help the leader-servant bring wholeness to others through reconciliation:

TOTAL FORGIVENESS DRIVES RECONCILIATION

As simple as forgiveness and unforgiveness may seem, there are several studies on the subject with often conflicting definitions. Unforgiveness involves holding back or keeping a record of emotional feelings (bearing grudges, bitterness, resentments, anger, malice, hurts or any form of injustice or unpaid debt) caused by someone else. Worthington (2005, 2006) [24, 25,] who has studied the subject extensively, broadly defined forgiveness as a "process of decreasing inter-related negative resentment-based emotions, motivations, and cognition." According to Worthington and others (2007), [26] "most researchers who studied transgressions by strangers or people in non-continuing relationships defined full (true) forgiveness as simply reducing unforgiveness, and researchers who studied continuing relationships defined full (true) forgiveness as decreasing and eventually eliminating unforgiveness by replacing the negative with positive and eventually building to a net positive forgiveness experience. These two sets of studies imply that forgiving people in a non-continuing relationship is different from forgiving a loved one. Worthington and his group concluded that forgiveness is of two types: a decision to control one's behaviors (i.e., decisional forgiveness) and a multifaceted sentimental forgiveness that involved changed cognition, passion, and motivation. [26] A combination of decisional forgiveness and emotional forgiveness is possible within my framework of a leader as servant leadership, although the two may have different pathways to true forgiveness.

Stating it simply, holding back those emotional feelings resulting from what another person or source (employer, government, or organization) did to you is unforgiveness, and releasing that person or source of the guilt of causing those feelings is forgiveness; it is canceling

Chapter 5
Developing Wholeness-Reconciliation

and letting those feelings or the record of them go. Unforgiveness could be of three sources or types: unforgiveness of self (self-condemnation), of others, and feeling of unforgiveness by God for the negative or sinful thing that one did that offended or hurt others or God. Forgiveness in each of these types may take different processes with different effects but the sum of true forgiveness in all of these (self, others, feeling forgiven by God) is what I will refer to as total forgiveness. It was an act of total forgiveness when Christ declared sinful humanity not guilty before God or by His act of love canceled the debt of death humanity owed to God. The Scripture says that love "Does not dishonor others, it is not self-seeking. It is not easily angered; it keeps no record of wrongs" (2 Corinthians 13:5, NIV). You have forgiven as an act of love when you keep no record of the wrongs done to you. In the context of the servant-leadership model, I posit that true forgiveness is a submissive obedient act of love whereby an offended chooses to transform his emotional perceptions to inside-out motivation not to count an offender's hurtful actions, offense, or debt in his feelings or relationship toward the offender; this must be done in a way that *glorifies* God. True forgiveness must include not only others, but the forgiver must also forgive themselves, and feel forgiven by God. God demands that we forgive each other (see Matthew 18:21-34; 1 Corinthians 13:4-7). It is difficult, if not impossible, to serve someone with whom you have hurt you have not let go.

Despite the Lord's command that we should forgive so that we will be forgiven, why is forgiveness so difficult, even for the best of Christian leaders? Lack of forgiveness is the major cause of divorce in Christian marriages. It is critical for a leader-servant to be ready to forgive to be a part of another's healing. Think of it this way: Take forgiveness as an action whereby you count your hurt as if it didn't happen (because Jesus has paid for it). Alternatively, take it as an action for which you refuse to remain a victim. On the other hand, better yet, choose to forgive to reap the full blessings of God's gift. By thinking of forgiveness in these terms, it will become as direct as obeying a commandment so important to our loving God that He made it the only condition by which He will forgive your trespasses. "And when ye stand praying, forgive, if ye have ought against any: that your Father also which is in heaven may forgive you your trespasses. However, if ye do not forgive, neither will your Father which is in heaven forgive your trespasses" (Mark 11:25-26, KJV).

Use this simple memory peg: For-Give = For-Go-Get Blessed. So, which is important: To forgive someone or not be forgiven by God? Truly, not forgiving is really a foolish shortsightedness that can affect one's health. Forgiveness opens the door to reconciliation. True forgiveness means that we might maintain our disapproval of what a person did or did not do, but relinquish the right for restitution from the offender and completely let go of the incident and all associated resentments. Forgiveness with reconciliation is really for our benefit because it is channeled through which God blessed us and through which we relate with God and rebuild broken relationships.

Forgiveness is not an act of excusing someone for an offense but more for the benefit of the forgiver's blessing as it is a condition for answered prayer and forgiveness from God who has the real power to judge. Forgiveness is not an act of reconciliation that requires two people to agree or forget the action, but true forgiveness occurs when we choose not to remember the action. Forgiveness is not approval, meaning you can forgive an action without approving it as Jesus showed in "Go and sin no more." John 8:11. Forgiveness is not pardoning or releasing someone from the consequence of an action; you cannot impose consequences or shield someone from God's dealing or the Law; forgiveness is not denying what was done; to truly forgive, you must acknowledge what was done; forgiveness is not forgetting the action.

True forgiveness is different from reducing unforgiveness. According to Worthington et al. (2007) [26] and Worthington (2001), [27] some common unforgiveness-reducing alternatives include:

(1) Seeing justice done
(2) Letting go and moving on
(3) Excusing an offense
(4) Justifying an offense
(5) Condoning an offense
(6) Forbearing
(7) Turning the issue over to God as a better judge
(8) Turning the issue to God for divine retribution.

However, I will state that true forgiveness can result from any of these unforgiveness-reducing alternatives when it emanates from an inside-out submissive obedient act of love that transforms the offended's emotional perception and motivates him or her not to count the discourtesy in feelings and relationships toward the offender; such an alternative will glorify God.

FORGIVING OTHERS THAT HURT YOU

When do you forgive? As Christ-like fruit! Should I forgive him? You do not require the aggravated to apologize for the offense before you forgive. It is not a choice but a commandment from God to be obeyed. As stated before; it is more to the benefit of the offended than the offender. However, most importantly, the lack of forgiveness is one simple pathway to Hell!

The most critical question is: how do we forgive? Forgiveness is directly related to wholeness, and yet some people remain in their hurts often because of pride or self-centeredness. Remember: forgiveness is the condition under which we are absolved and blessed by God. Nevertheless, there are situations where the leader, the Shepherd of God, is not on talking terms with followers. Because of accumulated hurts, the followers do not want to be distressed any further and do not want to relate to the leader. Some will actually leave the fellowship, church, or organization.

The health of an organization and its members is incumbent on the leader, no matter his hurt. The life story of Josh McDowell, author, and founder of Josh McDowell Ministries, a division of Campus Crusade for Christ, illustrates it best. The story was recounted in the movie, Undaunted: *The Early Life of Josh McDowell.* The film documented the effect Josh's lack of forgiveness from his father had on him as he was growing up. His father was a drunkard and routinely beat Josh's mother and hurt the entire family, both physically and emotionally, in the process. Josh said that his father hurt him so much in life that he enjoyed hating him. Once he feared he might forgive his father for all that he took him through. Josh, who was driven by the harsh reality of his life to prove that God did not exist, ended up certifying the opposite and later had an encounter with the living Christ. In response to his father's curiosity about why Josh forgave him for all he did to him, Josh said that since Jesus forgave his sin, he had to extend forgiveness to his father, who at the time was very sick in the hospital. Because of Josh's act of forgiveness, his father gave his life to Christ and was later healed. His father spent the rest of his life speaking about reconciliation, sharing how God healed him physically and mentally from alcoholism and healed him emotionally from his waywardness. His later focus in life was to reconcile with those he had hurt. That is a good example of wholeness and healing care, resulting from forgiveness and reconciliation. That was the example Jesus left for leader-servants to follow.

ACTS OF FORGIVING SELF

The first act of forgiving the self is letting go of self-condemnation. Unforgiveness of self is not letting go or emotionally keeping a record of your feelings for the hurt you caused to others or the sin you committed. It is allowing the guilt of those sins to always be in front of you and condemning you. It is the sense of self-condemnation from the belief that you have done something unforgivably wrong with others or sinned against God. Those feelings and the associated guilt and shame are stressful and unhealthy. You will not undergo totally forgiven until you deal with those feelings.

The process of forgiveness of self is clearly stated in the Scriptures. We read about God's call for forgiveness: "My people, who are called by My name will humble themselves and pray, and seek My face and turn from their wicked ways, then I will hear from heaven, will forgive their sin, and heal their land" (2 Chronicles 7:14, NKJV). God was addressing His people to humble themselves, to pray, and to repent to reconcile to Him. If we confess our sins, He is faithful and just to forgive us our sins and to cleanse us from all unrighteousness (1 John 1:9). Here is a biblically–based process for the forgiveness of self and freedom from feelings of unforgiveness from God:

| Confess | Humble yourself; seek the face and relationship with God that was broken by that sin; State in specific terms the truth of what you did; acknowledge your sin and the unjust or hurtful actions of yourself or your group toward others. |

Repent	See yourself as a sinner and hate your sin the same way God hates it. Turn away from sin or those actions with a heartfelt desire to change the behavior and attitude about what you did, forsake them, and return to loving actions not do it again by the grace of God through Christ.
Reconcile	Free yourself from sin condemnation and fully receive and accept forgiveness and pursue new intimate fellowship with those you have offended, starting with God; Live and walk in the Spirit to sustain that relationship with God and others;

- First, you must confess those sins before God and believe that He is faithful and just to forgive you of all sins, no matter how bad they are.
- Second, you must repent and forsake those sins.
- Third, you must begin to live and walk in the spirit of God.

You must believe that there is no more condemnation on you now that you walk and live in the spirit of God (Romans 12:1-2). Of course, the process assumes that you are in Christ Jesus, that is, you have accepted Him as your personal savior.

Cleansing and healing ourselves of these feelings go together. Healing or restoration to wholeness is a process that starts with humility, confession, repentance, and reconciliation. In relation to the health benefits of self-forgiveness, hypothesized that "self-condemnation may impair the self-care, produce depression and anxiety, and deactivate coping. That might result in more immediately apparent negative health consequences than the act of forgiving others" Worthington et al (2007).[27]

STRATEGIES FOR TRUE FORGIVENESS

Relinquish your right to get even. Start by letting the person who has hurt you off the hook: "Never avenge yourselves. Leave that to God, for he has said that he will repay those who deserve it" (Romans 12:19). The first step to forgiveness is committing not to take justice into your own hands. Let God be the impartial judge. One of the things I have learned in walking with God over the emotion of anger, especially toward my wife, was Him telling me, "you have no right unless the one I gave you, which is to unconditionally love my daughter, and no matter the right you think you have she is not giving you." In the process, I learned that I must only take Him seriously, and not my wife, not even myself. As difficult as that was, especially when I felt disrespected and absolutely correct, that voice would remind me, "you have no right to be upset." Such an attitude regulated my emotions toward anger and allowed me to channel my thought toward taking God seriously.

Reach out to others. Although Jesus could have focused on His own hurt and pain, on the cross, He chose to reach externally in love as a fellow sufferer and comfort others. "Today you will be with me in Paradise" (Luke 23:43). Job lost all his children and possessions but found healing and greater things after he prayed for his friends, including those that despised him (Job 42:10, 16). My younger brother from a different mother and his mother hurt me so much as we were growing up. His mother worked against me to complete my high school education and subjected me to very difficult challenges designed to discourage me. When my brother was sick, I had the opportunity to either get even with him or help him. Despite many people's advice to let him suffer; I chose to reach out to him and spent quite a lot of money on medical bills to bring healing to him. Before his mother died, she could not believe I did what I did to her son. She saw that God had blessed me despite all they did. I forgave her to bring healing to the relationships without requiring her apology. As we look below, Joseph in the Bible had the opportunity to get even with those that put him through so much pain and suffering, but he chose to reach out to them and love and empathy.

Release it to God. Our never-ending issues in life often make us ask, "How long Lord?" Nevertheless, real peace comes from committing those worries and their outcomes to God. When Jesus cried, "Father into your hands I commit my spirit" (Luke 23:46, NIV) It was an act of complete trust whereby he surrendered total control to His father. His prayer was; "not my will, but yours be done" (Luke 22:42, NIV). Jesus released it all to the Father. So, whatever we are facing today in life, in the aspect of despair and our deepest struggles, we must release all to God. Release it to God. Every time you remember how you've been hurt, release it. Jesus said: "Forgive 70 times seven" (Matthew 18:21-22, NIV). Does that mean 490 times? No, it means an unending number of perfections. In other words, we just keep forgiving each other, no limit intended. If you are slapped on one cheek, present the other cheek. If he slaps you on the second cheek, you still have the first cheek to present again. You will not run out of cheeks. You know you've released the pain when it doesn't hurt anymore. However, every time the pain comes to your mind, you say, "God, I give it to you again."

Refocus on your Servanthood. Concentrating on the hurt takes you away from your purpose of serving others to focusing on yourself. A servant leader's purpose is to relinquish his right to focus on serving others. He focuses more on the health of his relationship with the follower than the hurt. People are more likely to become what they focus on. You become a slave of what you make your master. Will you focus on the pain or the purpose of the service? You must refuse to be distracted and must focus on the purpose of your service as we read we learned from Job: "Put your heart right, reach out to God...then face the world again, firm and courageous. Then all your troubles will fade from your memory, like floods that are past and remembered no more" (Job 11: 13-16).

Replace and overcome the hurt with good. The Bible says, "Don't be overcome by evil, but overcome evil with good" (Romans 12:21, NIV). You don't overcome it by criticizing the offender. You overcome it with good to the offender or a positive attitude toward the offender. How do you know you are working on true forgiveness? Check out forgiveness in the life of Joseph in Genesis 37-45:1-15. To put this discussion in context, let us review the background. Joseph was one of the younger of 12 sons of Jacob. The youngest was Benjamin. His father loved him and spent more time with him because he was the son of his old age (Gen 37.3). His brothers became jealous of him because he was seen as his favorite son. Joseph had two prophetic dreams: In one, he was binding the sheaf of wheat grain with his brothers when his sheaf stood tall, and his brothers' sheaf bowed down to his. In the second dream, the sun and the moon, and eleven stars were bowing down to him (Genesis 37.9). When he shared the dreams with his brothers, they were insulted and plotted to kill him. Nevertheless, his oldest brother Reuben urged them not to kill him. His other older brother Judah suggested that they sell him into slavery to merchants going to Egypt, and they did. In Egypt, Joseph prospered in every challenge he faced and everything he did because the Lord was with him (Gen 39.23). Eventually, he became second in command to Pharaoh in all the affairs of Egypt, including being responsible for the management of food crops for the famine that came all over the land. So it was that Joseph's brother also came to Egypt to buy corn as "the whole world came to Egypt to buy corn from Joseph" (Gen 41.57).

Now put yourself in the position of Joseph in the presence of people who hated him enough to sell him into slavery, with clear intent to make him suffer. Could there be a worse enemy or a better opportunity for revenge? Joseph had all the rights, power, and privilege to get even with his brothers. However, he willingly chose to relinquish those rights to bring healing through forgiveness and reconciliation. Joseph in dealing with his brothers pursued the path, worthy of emulation by any leader-servant:

1. **He was prepared and private for the pain of forgiveness** (Genesis 45: 1-2). Leaders must be prepared for the true pain of forgiveness—letting go. Joseph was not willing to see outsiders see him overcome by his feelings, but cried out because of the hurt and the compassion he felt. It is okay that he wanted to keep the sins of his brethren as private as possible, even as God forgives our own trespasses, casting them into the depths of the sea (Micah 7:19). When we tell people of others' trespasses against us, what do we become? We become the judge. We want them punished, thereby acting as God who said: "Vengeance is Mine, I will repay say the Lord" (Romans 12:19). We also become the jury, setting the standard as our own judgment. God's perfect love drives away fears of punishment. We are to be kind loving and forgiving to each other as God forgives us (Ephesians 4:32).

2. **He was genuine and authentic** (Genesis 45: 3-4). Joseph did not appear intimidating and at the same time appear to show the act of forgiveness as some of us will be tempted to do. Joseph approached his brethren with love and compassion (Love drives away fears (1 John 4:18). Compare this with our usual approaches: we keep offended at a distance, but we forget that God does not keep us at arm's length. God does not bring our past to make us guilty for the present. He did not give us the spirit of fear, but of sound mind and son-ship (Romans 8:15). Joseph could have easily been puffed up by his success despite their sins against him or show his power and vindictiveness. Rather, Joseph revealed himself and his brothers' sin without passing any judgment,

excusing their actions, forgetting what they did, and so on, but in a non-threatening way.

3. **He avoided creating a guil trip for the offender** (Genesis 45:**5**). When we let the Holy Spirit work in the offender, it produces true repentance that helps in the forgiveness process. Joseph used the opportunity to honor God and gave Him glory. His act of forgiveness made it possible for his brothers to forgive themselves. One of Paul's greatest burdens was self-forgiveness for beheading the Christians. He was now ministering to the widows he created. Your guilt and self-pity will drag you down with bad taste; guilt can affect or even destroy your future relationships, steal your joy, and shorten your potential in some cases. Judas, Jesus' disciple who betrayed him for 30 pieces of silver, instead of asking for forgiveness, committed suicide due to guilt.

4. **He saw the sovereign act of God in the wickedness without approving the action** (Genesis 45:5-8). God sent Joseph before them and saved him to preserve their lives. He saved them from shame by showing the act of God. This is true forgiveness with love expressed. God elevated Joseph and made him the agent with which to accomplish His will. We could see the same pattern in the life of Jesus. Judas betrayed Jesus, but God elevated Jesus above all names. Joseph forgave from the heart with no place for self-righteousness because he saw God's hand at work in the bigger picture of things and meant well when he said, "You meant evil against me but God meant it for God. This indeed is true, total, and complete forgiveness. Forgiveness as a commandment from God needs to be done in the attitude of love of God. The process of forgiveness calls for us to have the mind of God and do it in the attitude of Love of God. (Romans 7:24; 1 Corinthians 13:4-7).

SUMMARY 5
DEVELOPING WHOLENESS-RECONCILIATION

Before starting this exercise, please read and follow the instruction in the preface of this workbook. Answers to these questions are contained in this chapter. Completion of these exercises after reading the chapter should take 60-90 minutes.

Discovering the Acts of wholeness-reconciliation

1. What is wholeness-reconciliation healing-care attitude? How did Jesus demonstrate wholes reconciliation in (Isaiah 53:5, NKJV) and yet in "Father forgive them, they do not know what they do..." (Luke 23:34).
2. How do you pursue and practice True Forgiveness
3. List key lessons from Joseph's handling of forgiveness
4. What are some of the health benefits of forgiveness and reconciliation

Principle of wholeness through True Forgiveness

1. How can the following principles help the leader-servant bring wholeness to others through reconciliation:
    a. Total Forgiveness Drives Reconciliation
    b. How is forgiveness as a "process of decreasing inter-related negative resentment-based emotions, motivations, and cognition." [26]
    c. How do you define True forgiveness (see Matthew 18:21-34; 1 Corinthians 13:4-7).
    d. why is forgiveness so difficult for people, even for the best of Christian leaders? Lack of forgiveness is the major cause of divorce in Christian marriages. (Mark 11:25-26, KJV).
    e. What are things that Forgiveness is not?
2. How is true forgiveness is different from reducing unforgiveness.[27] some common unforgiveness-reducing
3. The process of forgiveness calls for us to have the mind of God and do it in the attitude of Love of God. (Romans 7:24; 1 Corinthians 13:4-7).

CHAPTER 5
DEVELOPING WHOLENESS-RECONCILIATION

Practice of wholeness-reconciliation through True forgiveness

1. In the concept of "when enemies become friends." How is wholeness–reconciliation an act of harmonizing relationships and developing mutual respect between enemies to make them whole emotionally and relationally.
2. In Forgiving Others that Hurt You as a strategy for wholeness healing, when do you forgive? And how do we forgive?
3. What can we learn in the life story of Josh McDowell, author, and founder of Josh McDowell Ministries, a division of Campus Crusade for Christ, illustrates it bes?
4. The first act of forgiving the self is letting go of self-condemnation. What does the scripture teach about the process of forgiveness of self" (2 Chronicles 7:14, NKJV). (1 John 1:9).
5. How could the following Strategies for True Forgiveness be practiced
    a. **Relinquish your right to get even**. (Romans 12:19
    b. **Reach out to others**. (Luke 23:43). (Job 42:10, 16).
    c. **Release it to God**. (Luke 23:46, NIV)" (Matthew 18:21-22, NIV).
    d. **Refocus on your Servanthood**." (Job 11: 13-16).
    e. **Replace and overcome the hurt with good**. (Romans 12:21, NIV).
6. How do you know you are working on true forgiveness? Check out forgiveness in the life of Joseph in Genesis 37-45:1-15.
7. In what fours ways did Joseph willingly choose to relinquish those rights to bring healing through forgiveness and reconciliation. (Genesis 45: 1-2)." (Romans 12:19).

CHAPTER 6
DEVELOPING RELATIONAL WHOLENESS

We have often stated that leadership is about influence and the effectiveness of a leader to influence others toward a desired change depends on the relationship a leader has with others. Relational wholeness refers to the relationships between people or between a leader and his followers designed to make people and/or organizations complete and unified in a purpose. Ultimately, at the core of leadership is such a relationship. Jesus demonstrated his love toward his disciples and the established relationship He had with them created an opportunity for growth and the vision to see themselves in Him or His successors. Keeping the flock relationally together is an important responsibility of a leader servant. A healthy relationship allows the leader to know his followers and influences the follower to hear and follow the leader. Jesus said: "My sheep hear My voice, and I know them, and they follow Me" (John 10:27, NKJV). He emphasized such oneness in His prayers to the Father in John 17:1-13.

The relational wholeness can often be disrupted by sin, unforgiveness, conflicts and divisions between people or within the organization. To develop and sustain relational wholeness, the leader must work to resolve conflicts when they arise. The Scripture said, "What causes fights and quarrels among you? Don't they come from your desires that battle within you? You want something but don't get it. You kill and covet, but you cannot have what you want…You quarrel and fight" (James 4:1-4, NIV). Conflicts come from the different desires that battle in your heart; they are the direct results of disagreements due to differences and self-centeredness. They create divisions and are Devil's first tool to steal love between people and will invariably destroy their oneness if not timely resolved. No organization can thrive in the presence of unresolved conflicts and unhealthy relationships.

MANAGING MAJOR SOURCES OF CONFLICTS

Managing conflicts requires intentional other-centered actions for possible solutions. In Paul's exhortation in Colossians 3:12-19, the following key actions can be identified as strategies to guide achieving any resolution:

Focus more on your behavior changes. Our behavior changes start with a focus on putting bowels of mercies, kindness, humbleness of mind, meekness, and longsuffering (v. 12). This is a call to have "bowels" of opportunities at your disposal for mercies, kindness, humility, etc. applied toward positive attitudes to others. The Lord, in teaching the disciples on this issue instructed that we get the log out of our own eye first (Matthew 7:5); that is, examine, acknowledge, and work on your behavior that may be contributing to the conflict. Overlook minor offenses and talk over "big" offenses. We must use choose to use conflict as an opportunity to better understand each other.

Identify and define the specific conflict. There may be so many possible causes of a particular conflict but one or two may be the main issue leading to others. That needs to be identified as the primary cause of the conflict. This is where the leader-servant serve as both a counselor and a minister of peace. As a counselor, the leader leads his followers to find out, together, what the major issue is. It may be too presumptuous to guess why the other is upset. He will lead them to define the specific reason for the conflicts. All must work together in an atmosphere of selfless love to identify the real issue and why and how this issue is causing a conflict. Oftentimes, understanding the real issue creates opportunities to understand each other. Because what one person may see as a serious problem may not be for the other and that in itself causes conflict. Each person must be willing to own up to the behaviors the other person sees as contributing to the conflict. Until each person identifies the problem he or she has and is willing to accept responsibility or contribution to it, they are not ready for a solution or resolution. As a minister, he works separately to attend to the emotional hurts caused by the conflict, minister and lead the way to pursue minister and communicate with those involved that without such peace the house of God is divided and no one shall see God.

THE SIX STAGES OF CONFLICT RESOLUTION

There are six stages of identifying and resolving conflict—Problem, Feeling, Need and Desire, Solution, Reconciliation, and Commitment stages.

1) **Problem Identification Stage.** Identify the primary issue or problem causing the conflict:
2) **Feeling Identification Stage-**Identify everybody' positions and emotional feelings about the problem or issue (Ephesians 4:26-32)
3) **Need and Desire Identification Stage--**Identify what the needs and desires are to completely resolve the issue and fully restore the relationship (James 4:1-4).
4) **Solution Identification Stage:** Identify possible solutions, alternative solutions, and possible compromises
5) **Reconciliation Stage.** Seek and pursue genuine reconciliation. Reconciliation brings healing to the conflict and wholeness to the broken relationship
6) **Commitment Stage.** The rule is: To agree and commit with specific actions toward a solution = Resolution

The problem revealed is the problem half-solved; the required behavioral change becomes clear to all when problems caused by the behaviors are revealed; changes are needed in all involved since all share in the contributions to the conflict. Many possible alternative solutions may need to be identified. The goal is to find a mutually acceptable solution out of the identified alternative solutions and be willing to make needed compromises to decide the best way forward with a specific implementation plan toward the desired behavioral change for all involved.

There may be some compromises. In compromising, each must expect to lose something for all to gain something that restores all together. Compromise in the solution stage is the beginning of reconciliation that yields commitment to permanent resolution. To pursue genuine reconciliation, you must forgive totally to open the way for genuine reconciliation; you must remember that forgiveness is a spiritual process that you cannot fully accomplish on your own without God; you must "Bear with each other and forgive whatever grievances you may have against one another.

You must forgive as the Lord forgave you" (Colossians 3:12-14; see also 1 Corinthians. 13:5; Psalm 103:12; Isaiah. 43:25). Willingness to make a mutually agreeable compromise is very important to a resolution. But until a commitment is made and agreed to by all parties, the resolution will not be achieved. With the heart of reconciliation, these actions make more sense, and commitments to them will now fall on healthy forgiven hearts.

Also from the Lord's teaching, we must remember the following reconciliatory actions:

Get the log out of your own eye first

A log is a typical blind spot that impedes the correct evaluation of a situation (Matthew 7:5). There are two kinds of "logs":

(1) Critical, negative, or overly sensitive attitude that leads to unnecessary conflict. You get rid of this log by spending some time meditating on the good of your spouse and_adopting the kind of attitude that avoids conflict (Philippians 4:8-9).

(2) Hurtful words and actions are the second logs. This type of log is removed by taking an objective look at yourself, facing up to your contribution to a conflict, identifying ways that you have wronged the other, and admitting your wrongs honestly and thoroughly.

Overlook minor offenses

An offense should be overlooked if you can answer "no" to all of the following questions: (1) Is the offense seriously dishonoring God? (2) Has it permanently damaged a relationship?; (3) Is it seriously hurting other people? And, (4) is it seriously hurting the offender or victim? If you answer "yes" to any of these questions, an offense is too serious to overlook. Actions to take include:

- Go and talk with the "offender" privately and lovingly about the situation (see Matthew. 18:15).
- In that case, plan your words carefully; be specific and to the point, Assume the best about your mate until you have facts to prove otherwise (Proverb 11:27);
- Each should readily admit each person's contribution to a conflict and Clearly apologize (see Proverb 19:11);

- Speak only to build the other up. Test what you say (see Table 3.1) and how you say it: is it immoral, debasing, edifying, and graceful? Paul said it best: "Let no corrupt communication proceed out of your mouth, but that which is good to the use of edifying, that it may minister grace unto the hearers" (Ephesians 4:29)

Create a climate of peace in your home

Creating a climate for peace will require your understanding of the 4 peaceable P's;

(1) **Peaceable Perspective**. The good in others must be our perspective. Our focus should be to work with an open mind and positive attitude to find the good things in people and base our relationship on those things. Our positive attitude can be a pathway to the peace we seek. Paul said: "whatsoever things are true, whatsoever things are honest, whatsoever things are just, whatsoever things are pure, and whatsoever things are lovely… think on these things."

(2) **Peaceable Process**. Creating a long-lasting peaceable relationship is a process of submitting to and understanding one another in all things (Ephesians 5:21). It is a process that may start roughly at the beginning but we must keep submitting and respecting each other as a way to break down attitude the devil can use to cause conflicts.

(3) **Peaceable Problems**. How can a problem be peaceable? By seeing the inevitable problems in a relationship as indispensable growth opportunities, the conflict presents choice opportunities for growth and understanding, and the victories in those problems bring Glory to God. Thus, to sustain peace in that "difficult situation", according to Romans 12:18, our love must be more than an act of our will. It is based on God's covenant and command to love (1 Corinthians 13:4-8).

(4) **Peaceable Pardon**. To sustain peace means that we must commit to being kind… Forgiving and forbearing one another (Ephesians 4:32, Colossians 3:13).

HEALTH BENEFITS AND EFFECTS OF FORGIVENESS

One of the most comprehensive reviews of the health benefits of forgiveness can be found in the recent review article and other works of Worthington et al.(2007) [28] and Williams (2003). [29] Included in the review are studies on forgiveness and peripheral physiology with a focus on the emotional processes potentially related to forgiveness and physical health. In the study by Toussaint and Williams (2003) [29] cited in the above review, the blood pressure of a diverse sample of 100 mid-western community residents was measured to determine the effect of forgiveness on blood pressure. According to these researchers, higher levels of total forgiveness were associated with lower resting diastolic blood pressure across participants. The study also revealed differences separated by socioeconomic status and race: among white participants of high socioeconomic status, total forgiveness and forgiveness of self were associated with lower resting diastolic blood pressure. Forgiveness of others was associated with lower resting diastolic blood pressure among black participants with low socioeconomic status, and forgiveness of others, total forgiveness, and perceived divine forgiveness were associated with lower resting cortisol levels. The combined results according to these authors suggest that "chronic unforgiving responses could contribute to adverse health by perpetuating stress beyond the duration of the original stressor. By contrast, forgiving responses may buffer health both by quelling these unforgiving responses and by nurturing positive emotional responses in their place." [28]

In addition to spiritual and emotional healing, and meeting the condition of answered prayers, forgiveness has some other research-based physical health benefits. We have learned from studies by Lawler et al. (2003), [29], and other studies that forgiveness can be associated with lower heart rate, blood pressure, and stress relief. These studies concluded that forgiveness can bring long-term health benefits for your heart and overall health. Similar follow-up studies by the same group found that forgiveness can be positively associated with five measures of health: physical symptoms, use of medications, sleep quality, fatigue, and somatic complaints. [29] These researchers noted the importance of emotional forgiveness in reducing unforgiveness. Through forgiveness, one can experience a reduction in negative effects (depressive symptoms), a strengthened spirituality, improved conflict management, and stress relief. All of these have a significant beneficial impact on overall health. Forgiveness not only restores positive thoughts, feelings, and behaviors toward the offending party but restores the relationship to its previous positive state. [30]

PURSUE RECONCILIATION FOR LASTING PEACE

True reconciliation is an important dimension of wholeness healing. It is a process that starts with genuine forgiveness and ends with total inside-out cleansing. To be free from accusation means to heal the hurting souls of friends who have allowed their relationships to deteriorate to that of being enemies.

It is not the conflict or the sin that caused the deterioration of the relationship but the lack of forgiveness. Reconciliation opens the door to love and being loved again without fear. Without reconciliation, forgiveness alone will not bring unity and prosperity in the work of God. Wholeness will not be completely restored without true reconciliation. This is the kind of love and forgiveness that God wants us to show to others. Jesus died to reconcile us to God. Joseph established lasting peace with his brothers through genuine reconciliation. Good marriages last for a long time not because couples are perfect, but because when in crisis, the couple can reconcile by working together to build passionate stability (See Genesis 11:1-9; Acts 4: 31-34). Several lessons from these scriptures can be noted: Satisfied intimacy builds your strengths and reduces emotions; better understanding increases knowledge of each other; mutual sentimental, physiological, and physical understanding yields more tolerance; evaluating the outcome of individual actions and making changes if necessary build emotional stability.

HOW TO ACHIEVE RECONCILIATION

Apologize to reconcile

This is important if the offense was perpetrated by the leader-servant. What does the Bible say about an apology or apologizing? It says nothing that directly addresses the method of apologizing! However, we learn about apologizing by studying the words "confession," "forgiveness," "repentance," and "reconciliation." We can also take a look at some situations in the Bible where elements of apologizing took place and what the outcomes of apologizing were.

Real and meaningful apologies are a cry within us for reconciliation. A purposeless apology can actually make reconciliation difficult and must be avoided. Meaningless apologies are often given to benefit the offender in some way rather than helping the victim feel better. It may also be an attempt to blame the sufferer for the victimization or an attempt to turn around the situation and accuse the victim of causing the offense. Alternatively, an apology may be given because the abuser now wants or needs something from the offended or can be offered simply to silence the victim, move on, and avoid anyone else learning about the offense or betrayal.

Some elements of a relevant apology include ensuring that the words are authentic and heartfelt. The offender accepts responsibility for the wrongdoing; it is focused on the victim's feelings rather than those of the offender; it attempts to bring healing to the victim; it is delivered in a humble and non-patronizing way; the injured feels genuine commitment by the offender not to do the same thing again; and no excuses or attempts are made to cause the offended to feel guilty.

A meaningful apology must be concerned primarily with righting the wrong and is given to make it crystal clear that the victim's feelings are the offender's top priority. An apology can also show remorse for the pain the offense caused, the ramifications of the behavior, and how it affected the victim's life.

Apologies are beneficial but not a requirement.

We can also recall Jonah's heartfelt apology to God for his disobedience. As a result, God had the fish spit Jonah out on dry land, and thus Jonah was given a second chance (see Jonah chapter 2). Joseph's brothers sold him into slavery. Instead, Joseph was favored by God and man; His brothers apologized for what they had done to Joseph. Joseph and his brothers were reconciled after some heartfelt apologies. We also see how God allowed Devil to inflict Job physically and financially. Job apologized to God for speaking about things he did not understand. It wasn't until this apology happened that God healed Job and restored his finances (Job Chap 42). And many other examples! In Genesis (32,

33), Jacob tricked Esau into giving him his birthright and then stole his father's blessing. Jacob offered Esau a sincere apology along with many gifts. Esau forgave his brother and did not kill him like he had said he would earlier. Jacob received forgiveness and got to keep his life because he apologized.

An apology also helps the offended receive healing for the hurt and a blessing from God for forgiving the offender. Both the offender and the victim (offended) are reconciled, and the relationship is restored and strengthened. Joseph's brothers' relationship with Joseph was restored. Being answerable for what you have done is the true test of maturity in a leader-servant. Being accountable for your behavior means repentance, restitution, and personal responsibility. Some promises you can make when you forgive someone include: I will be settled in my mind that the incident is over; I will not bring this incident up and use it against you; I will not allow this incident to stand between us or hinder our relationship and work for God. In those actions, it is important to keep in mind what forgiveness is not: It is not an approval or to show that what happened did not hurt. It simply means that you can forgive an action without approving it or denying the hurt (John 8:11).

Even with its benefits, why is apologizing hard for some? When apologizing feels difficult to an offender, it may mean that the offender has not really owned up to the responsibility of the offense; the offender may not be tender or showing care enough about the feelings of the victim and reconciliation of the relationship; the risk of being ridiculed for the offense; alternatively, the risk of rebuff and humiliation if the other person rejects the apology and refuses to forgive. Apologizing, then, can require a great deal of courage. The risk of being viewed as the instigator of unpleasantness can initiate a feeling of guilt. I believe that pride and arrogances are the main reason people find it difficult to readily apologize. An apology is God's command as part of repentance, forgiveness, and reconciliation to bring healing. This is an imperative call for action for the healing of the victim and offender and requires humility and boldness.

HUMILITY AS A SERVANT

Humility from a servant's heart initiates the acts of reconciliation. Only a heart of humility like in the case of Jesus or Joseph, in this case, will allow an offended to relinquish his rights to see a broken relationship healed. I believe the relationship Joseph had with his father, and his love for, and authenticity with his brothers, drove his actions for reconciliation. Building an authentic relationship is an important element of effective leadership. Looking at Joseph's life again as an example with respect to reconciliation (Genesis 45:9-15), we can learn the following lessons:

Offended helps the offender deal with the regret, repentance, and forgiveness (Genesis 45: 9-15). Joseph helped his brothers deal with the guilt, regret, and self-forgiveness; Joseph chose to dwell only on the positive work of God in the situation; and Joseph's complete forgiveness is exemplified by his unconditional reinstatement of their relationship.

Offended and offenders work together to build each other's strength. Lasting relationships work together to build each other's strength (spiritual, emotional, and physical strengths) by adopting a good character; increasing security in the relationship builds trust and confidence.

The offended empties the hurt to reconcile and bond again with the offender. Hurts break the bond that holds relationships together. In order to reconcile, we must empty the hurts and clean ourselves inside out to bond and relate again. True reconciliation takes place when the two begin to enjoy intimate fellowship with each other, which is made possible only through the cross of Jesus Christ. On the cross, Jesus healed the broken hearts of His followers and mankind by reconciling humanity to the Heavenly Father. He also commissioned His followers to the ministry of reconciliation in the world. The lessons learned from the Calvary cross include:

Offended bears his cross and expends himself toward the offender. Jesus expected his followers to bear their own crosses. He said; "Take up your cross and follow Me" (Matthew 16:24, NKJV) - as a way of empowering His followers to be healers and reconcilers by enduring any pain for the sake of service toward others. To quote Pastor Lance, "Leaders must commit to spending themselves instead of spending on themselves." This means acts of reconciliation begin with God. We must invest in the health of others more so than in ourselves. If we are not fully harmonized with God, we cannot reconcile with others. Our relationship with others is as good as we make our relations with God. When the relationship is healthy, it empowers and secures us to heal other relationships. To be reconciled to God, we must openly acknowledge and confess our sins to be cleansed and forgiven; indeed, covering up sins bring down judgment. A leader-servant's responsibility is to lead his followers to follow; "Confess your faults one to another that you may be healed" (James 5:16)

In all of these examples, Joseph, who was offended and sold into slavery, initiated the acts of reconciliation. He gave up his rights for an apology. Rather, he saw the hand of God in the offense. That is an essential action expected by a leader-servant as demonstrated also by Jesus through our ministry. Joseph was a good reconciler, and we must humble ourselves enough to emulate his examples to bring healing to others.

Be the reconciler to reconcile.

As I was looking for good reconcilers in our world today, I came across an article by John Dawson of International Reconciliation Ministry. In his book, *"What Christians Should Know about Reconciliation,"* [31] he recounted how to "walk out" of reconciliation. He had to move his Anglo family into the African-American community in Los Angeles. He identified with the struggles of this community and developed meaningful friendships there. In one of his travels, he sat next to an African American grandmother on an airplane and took the opportunity to ask for forgiveness for the sins of his people. The grandmother was cool to him early on but later opened up and shared how her own great-grandmother was sold at age 8 at a slave auction in Richmond, Virginia. Eventually, they fully connected and the conversation changed when she heard that John had lived for 20 years in an African community and that they shared many things in common in this community. This is an outstanding example of an authentic reconciler. It took commitment and conviction to make such a move. John wrote,

> As Christians, it should be our hope that our children will not have to deal with the hatred and alienation that have marked this and previous generations because of devilish strongholds rooted in history. Let us identify the ancient and modern wounds of injustice, pride, and prejudice in our world and

biblically heal them, without self-righteous accusations or dishonest cover-ups.[31]

A leader-servant is called to be a reconciler of his followers not only to God but to each other, confessing faults one to another to bring healing and wholeness to the body. The Scripture says; "Make every effort to live in peace with everyone and to be holy; without holiness, no one will see the Lord" (Hebrews 12:14, NIV). We are called to make every effort that includes taking intentional steps to forgive and be forgiven and renewing a relationship to be at peace with people.

Be an intercessor to reconcile

During the darkest days of the American Civil War, Abraham Lincoln summoned the people. He proclaimed the following words:

> ... recognize the hand of God in this terrible visitation, to the remembrance of our own faults and crimes as a nation and as individuals, to humble ourselves before Him and to pray for His mercy - to pray that we may be spared further punishment, though most justly deserved... it is the duty of nations as well as of men, to own their independence upon the overruling power of God; to confess their sins and transgressions in humble sorrow; yet with assured hope that genuine repentance will lead to mercy and pardon." (President Lincoln gave a warning in his proclamation of March 30, 1863).[32]

This is a president who is acting as an intercessor. These words could as well have come from the notes of the preacher. Just like John the Baptist, he was saying confess, repent, and be healed. One wonders why today's leaders are either ashamed of using the name of God or evoking the power of God. Or are they simply pagans in the practice of religiosity?

Be an imitator of Christ

Leader-servants can emulate the ultimate leader-servant: Jesus Christ. The purpose of His Calvary Cross is the reason for your existence to be used to reconcile others. Your Calvary cross is any state of suffering and distress you experience as a child of God. He was an empathetic healer through reconciliations.

He suffered for the remission of our sins. "(He) gave himself for our sins, that he might deliver us from this present evil world, according to the will of God and our Father" (Galatians 1:4). So, as a leader just like Jesus, you must be humble yourself and endure an insult from a friend or a family member or forgiven a family member of that BIG sin? His Calvary cross must yield in us a mind to suffer any hurt and be an example for others. He suffered to demonstrate His love in that; "For when we were yet without strength, in due time Christ died for the ungodly...But God commended his love toward us, in that, while we were yet sinners, Christ died for us" (Romans 5:6-8). This challenges us to see love as a covenant commandment that we must demonstrate to all people regardless of the response or action of the receiver. We must be able to demonstrate that to others through examples.

He suffered for our reconciliation, to bring all to God since he; "… made peace to reconcile all things unto himself; to present you holy and blameless in his sight" (Colossians 1:20-22). This means that there is no limit to the extent you must go to bring peace into any Godly relationship, especially those in the household of God, beginning with your family. We must triumph over the devil's stronghold that affects our peace. Jesus already; "…spoiled principalities and powers, he made a show of them openly, triumphing over them in it" (Colossians 2:15).

SUMMARY 6
DEVELOPING RELATIONAL WHOLENESS

Before starting this exercise, please read and follow the instruction in the preface of this workbook. Answers to these questions are contained in this chapter. Completion of these exercises after reading the chapter should take 60-90 minutes.

Discovering Relational Wholeness-Healing Care

1. What is Relational wholeness?

2. What did Jesus teachin about relational wholeness when He us said: "My sheep hear My voice, and I know them, and they follow Me" (John 10:27, NKJV) as in John 17:1-13.
3. What disrupts relational wholeness that we must avoid? (James 4:1-4, NIV). How does conflict affect relationship

Principle

1. True reconciliation is an important dimension of wholeness healing. Wholeness will not be completely restored without true reconciliation. How did Jesus demonstrate this principle Joseph established lasting peace with his brothers through genuine reconciliation. (See Genesis 11:1-9; Acts 4: 31-34). What other lessons or principles can be learned from these examples
2. How do the following strategies Achieve Reconciliation
   a. Apologize to reconcile
   b. Apologies are beneficial but not a requirement.
   c. Be the reconciler to reconcile.

Practicing Acts of Relational wholeness

1. In Paul's exhortation in Colossians 3:12-19, how can the following key intentional other-centered actions be used to for managing conflicts
   a. **Focus more on your behavior changes.**
   b. **Identify and define the specific conflict.**
2. Identify the six stages of identifying and resolving conflict. State the reconciliation resolution rule .
3. From the Lord's teaching, how do we practice the following reconciliatory actions:
   a. **Get the log out of your own eye first**
   b. **Overlook minor offenses**
   c. **Create a climate of peace in your home**
4. What are some Health Benefits and Effects of Forgiveness
5. In his book, *"What Christians Should Know about Reconciliation,"* [31] he recounted how to "walk out" of reconciliation.. John wrote,

> *As Christians, it should be our hope that our children will not have to deal with the hatred and alienation that have marked this and previous generations because of devilish*

strongholds rooted in history. Let us identify the ancient and modern wounds of injustice, pride, and prejudice in our world and biblically heal them, without self-righteous accusations or dishonest cover-ups. [31]

a. What exactly are we called to do in this example and in the scriptures (Hebrews 12:14, NIV).
b. **Be an intercessor to reconcile**
c. **Be an imitator of Christ**

Chapter 7
Developing the Acts Healing-Care Comfort

Healing-care comfort means to aid someone who is "cast down" or in any kind of trouble to bring wellness to that person or alleviate the excessive sorrow the person might be going through (2 Corinthian 2:7). We are comforted by God so that we may be able to console others in trouble (2 Corinthians 1:2-4). What does it mean to comfort others? Especially when encouraged or to reassure others? We are expected to comfort others with the same comfort we receive from God. What, then, are the comforts we receive from God? How do we comfort others? These reflective questions are worthy of consideration.

Sorrows that Need Comforting

Typical sorrow that needs comforting can be one of three possible kinds (2 Corinthians 7: 8-10):

(1) Leader-inflicted sorrow on others (corrections, convictions, condemnations from truth of what the leader said in love, etc.);

(2) Godly good sorrow that works repentance to salvation (broken spirit, repentance for sin, contrite spirit); and

(3) world-sorrow that works death (such as unrepentant sorrow, pain over a loss, grief, lack of pleasure, punishment, bondage, homelessness, bareness, betrayal, etc.). Other sorrows could be self-inflicted dreadful sorrow, which is caused by bad choices, including leader-inflicted sorrow such as abuse (emotional and verbal) or burden-sorrow caused by obligations (good and bad). This can be likened to the sorrow Jesus felt in the Garden of Gethsemane; "My soul is overwhelmed with sorrow to the point of death" (Matthew 26: 38) Jesus' disciples fell asleep, "exhausted from sorrow" or by their grief (Luke 22:45).

(4) The direct impact of comfort is to bring wholeness by removing the unhealthy bad sorrow (2 Corinthians 7:10) or helping someone deal with good sorrow that leads to the intended purpose in God. The primary purpose of comfort may not always be to completely remove the trouble such as those caused by sickness or accident but to ease the sorrow caused by the trouble or to prepare the mind to deal with the sorrow. In the case of Jesus, we read that the angel came and strengthened Him to ease His sorrow (Luke 22:43) but did not remove the burden.

STRATEGIES OF CONFRONTING OTHERS

Some ways we can comfort others through the comfort we receive from God include the following:

Comfort with ordinary human emotions

Comfort others with ordinary human emotions and feelings. The sorrow a leader brings to his followers must be measured by its impact and how the sufferer is strengthened with ordinary human emotions and feelings. Is the sorrow a vindictive act burnout of desire for revenge to get even or hurt someone? The impact of the sorrow will not lead to Godly sorrow (repentance) if the benefit of the sorrow does not lead to regret. The benefit of Godly sorrow includes things such as leading someone to repentance, based on God's will; working out of obedience; a desire to make things correct; cleansing of the self from sin; zeal to do the right things, and so on. We can regret the pain of the godly sorrow we cause but rejoice in the benefits those sorrows bring to the sufferer (2 Corinthians 7:3-10). We are to cry with those who cry and mourn with those that mourn as our basic human emotions and feelings.

Comfort others by showing Love

The most life-changing action we can take is to speak the corrective truth to others in love. Paul, in his letter to the Corinthian church, acknowledged that his words were strong but did not regret that he spoke them in love. He rejoiced with them for the impact of his words and affirmed that he had confidence in them in all things.

CHAPTER 7
DEVELOPING THE ACTS HEALING-CARE COMFORT

That must have been encouraging to them to hear this from a leader they respected. However, the most important lesson for leaders, in this case, was that Paul could follow through to assess the impact of his words and reassure his readers of his love and intentions. In so doing, Paul showed that he cared for them. He explained the reason for his letter, "That our care for you in the sight of God might appear to you… Therefore, we have been comforted in your comfort" (2 Corinthians 7:15-16).

Comfort from the comfort received from God

Comfort others with empathy and comfort from God. Leaders are great comforters when they express and channel their feelings of emotions, empathy, and comfort from what they get from the Lord. David for example; usually found comfort and empathy from the promises of God. He said, "Why are you cast down, O my inner self? Hope in God and wait expectantly for Him, for I shall yet praise Him, my Help and my God" (Psalm 42:5) and "You have turned my mourning into dancing for me…" (Psalm 30:11). He expressed feelings of depression and sorrow and yet found comfort in the awareness that God was his chief empathize. The Apostle Paul acknowledged possible feelings of fear, frustration, anxiety, and weakness. However, he rested on the assurance that strength in Jesus is made perfect in his weaknesses. We see in these two leaders' expressions different kinds of feelings from sadness, fear, sorrow, and anxiety to desires for love. These examples also suggest ways to control these emotions, including hope in God, prayer and supplications, Thanksgiving, walking by the spirit, and casting down sinful imaginings. People can experience what they express to others. You experience love in a relationship if you deposit more love actions into that space. An expression of love creates a culture of love. Having a clear sense of your emotions and feelings is critical in developing empathy to comfort others.

Comfort as obedience to the Father's Will

Servant leadership is all about service to others according to the purposes of God. At Cavalry Cross, Jesus voluntarily laid down His life. So, just a leader-servant lay down his or her life to healing the hurting world (Matthew 27:50)? Jesus saw the complete work of salvation as more important than His life or will. He voluntarily released it all to the Father. Thus, a leader-servant must lead others through the process of reconciliation.

Comfort as caregiver

Leader-servants comfort to take care of people who depend on them. Jesus, in his own hurt, also recognized and acknowledged the hurt of his mother, her need to be comforted, and to have a protective covering of a son. At Calvary, He declared, "Woman beholds thy son, son beholds thy mother" (John 19:26-27, NKJV). He did not let his suffering blind him to the needs of those that depended on him. Likewise, you must let people around know your hurt but do not let them suffer because you are suffering (Philippians 2:3-8). Paul wants us to bring comfort to others, "Let the mind of self-emptying be in you, which was in Christ" (Philippians 2:5, NIV).

SUMMARY 7
DEVELOPING THE ACTS HEALING-CARE COMFORT

Before starting this exercise, please read and follow the instruction in the preface of this workbook. Answers to these questions are contained in this chapter. Completion of these exercises after reading the chapter should take 60-90 minutes.

Discovering the Acts of Healing-Care Comfort

Healing Care-Comfort- means to aid someone who is "cast down" or in any kind of trouble "so that he will not be overwhelmed by excessive sorrow".
1. How is comforting someone an act of empathy?
2. What does Healing-care comfort mean?
3. What does the bible teach about Healing-care conform? (2 Corinthian 2:7). (2 Corinthians 1:2-4).
4. What, then, are the comforts we receive from God?
5. What are the kinds of sorrows that needs comforting (2 Corinthians 7: 8-10; Matthew 26: 38; Luke 22:43-45).

Practicing Acts of healing-Care comfort

1. What are some ways to achieve this?
2. How does the Lord comfort us?
3. How do you comfort others?
6. How can the following strategies be used to comfort others through the comfort we receive from God
7. Comfort with ordinary human emotions (2 Corinthians 7:3-10).
8. Comfort others by showing Love 2 Corinthians 7:15-16).
9. Comfort from the comfort received from God
10. Comfort others with empathy and comfort from God. L (Psalm 42:5) (Psalm 30:11).
11. Comfort as obedience to the Father's Will ((Matthew 27:50)?
12. Comfort as caregiver (John 19:26-27, NKJV)." (Philippians 2:5, NIV).
13. Based on the questions in Table 5, can you identify each of the acts of healing-care leadership attribute? What ones did you score 3 ("sometimes") or less than 3? Review and learn and commit to work to improve.

ALS HEALING-CARE LEADERSHIP ATTRIBUTES, PRINCIPLES, & PRACTICES

Table 5. Leadership Healing-Care Attribute Audit

Servant leadership healing care attribute is the combined acts of providing comfort and empathy to make others whole emotionally and spiritually Assess the quality of your acts of healing care attribute by inserting an X below the number that best describes your response to each statement.

Item	Acts of Healing Care Attribute Check 1= Always; 2= Frequently; 3= Sometimes; 4= Almost Never; 5= Never	1	2	3	4	5
1	I have the emotional and spiritual capacity to comfort myself and others					
2	I act in ways to build up and support the wholeness of others					
3	I Invite the presence of God into the healing process through fervent prayers.					
4	I develop a sense of oneness and obligation to meet the healing-wholeness of others					
5	I comfort my followers and assure them of their self-worth					
6	I walk through with others in their own state of suffering.					
7	I provide comfort and empathy to make others whole emotionally and spiritually					
8	My sense of personal healing affect my inner strength to face challenges competently and to help others,					
9	I continuously gauge my action and their impact on others					
10	My self-healing or wholeness of others begins with total forgiveness and reconciliation					
11	**Add up your rating in each column**					
Score Range	Guide and Explanation of Score: understand the areas you need to further develop	Score				
10-17	Great Healing care leadership; keep it up!					
18-25	Above Average Healing Care; need to work on 25% of the areas					
26-33	Average for greatness; need to work on 50% of the areas					
34-41	Below average- healing care, need to work on 75% of the areas					
42-50	No healing care leadership ; work in all the areas					

TOPIC INDEX

About This Book, 22
Acts of Forgiving Others, 79, 87
Acts of Forgiving Self, 80, 87
Affective Compassion, 75, 86
affirmations, 72
authentic, 24, 26
authentic leadership, 37
Authentic Leadership, 45
Authenticity, 43
Comfort, 41, 106, 107, 109
commitment, 19, 25
Comparisons
   with other works, 40
credibility, 48
Discipleship
   definition of, 27
Discovering the Act of Generosity-Giving, 72
distinguishes
   a leader's act of giving, 29
Functional Definitions, 35
Generosity
   definition of, 29
Generosity c, 29
giving, 29
   habit of, 29
HEALING CARE-COMFORT, 108
Healing-Comfort, 108
Health Benefits and Effects of Forgiveness, 94
How to Achieve Reconciliation, 95, 102
Imitator of Christ, 100
inside-out, 46
intentional actions, 70, 73
Joshua, 19
law of, 42
Leader as Servant Leadership, 42
   definition, 25
Leader First., 23

Leader-as-Servant Leadership, 23
leader-servant's affection-attribute
   definition, 48
leadership, 25
Leadership Attributes, 43
Leadership Inner Value system, 25
Model, 23
Moses, 19
Navigation-attribute, 48
Organizational leadership trust, 32
Personal Outward Authenticity, 47
Practicing Servant Leadership
   Healing Care, 57
process, 25
Reconciliation, 81, 95, 101, 116
Seek self-healing, 58, 66, 110
Self-Healing
   definition, 58, 66, 110
sense of oneness, 58, 64, 67, 110
sense of purpose, 65, 67
sense of self-efficacy, 65, 67
Servant, 23, 24
state of suffering, 73
Strategies
   for True Forgiveness, 81, 87
Strategies for forgiving others
      Refocus on your servanthood, 83
      Overcome the Hurt with good, 83
      Refocus on your servanthood, 87
      Overcome the Hurt with good, 87
test
   for leader-servant authenticity, 46
   of essential elements of personal authenticity, 46, 47
The Leadership Healing Care-Attribute, 58, 110
The Leadership Influence-attribute, 41
the presence of God, 58, 64, 67, 110
Total Forgiveness, 76, 86

REFERENCES

[1]Greenleaf, R. (1970). *The Servant as Leader,* Indianapolis: The Robert K. Greenleaf Center

[2]Spears, L. (1996*).* "*Reflections on Robert K. Greenleaf and servant-leadership.*" Leadership & Organization Development Journal, 17(7), 33-35

[3]Russell, R.F. (2001). "The role of values in servant leadership." *Leadership & Organization Development Journal,* 22(2), 76-83

[4]Russell, R.F., and Stone, A.G. (2002). "A review of servant leadership attributes: developing a practical model." *Leadership & Organization Development Journal,* 23(3), 145-15

[5]Terry. R. W (1993*). Authentic Leadership: Courage In Action,* San Francisco, CA ,Jossey-Bass

[6]George, B (2003). *Authentic Leadership: Rediscovering the Secrets to Creating Lasting Value.* San Francisco, CA, Jossey-Bass

[7]Shamir, B. & Eilam, G. (2005). "What's your story? Toward a life-story approach to authentic leadership." Leadership Quarterly, 16, 395–418.

[8]Anderson, GL (2009). Advocacy Leadership: Toward a Post-Reform Agenda in Education, Routledge, New York, 41

[9]Yacobi, B.G. *"Elements of Human Authenticity."* http://www.philosophytogo.org /wordpress/?p=1945, Retrieved, July 15, 2012

[10]George, B (2003). *Authentic Leadership: Rediscovering the Secrets to Creating Lasting Value*, San Francisco, CA, Jossey-Bass

[11]Wosu, SN (2014), *Leader as Servant Leadership Model,* Xulon Press

[23]*Kanov*, J.M., S. Maitlis, M.C. Worline, J.E., Dutton, P.J.Frost, & J.M. Lilius (2004)"Compassion in organizationallife.' American Behavioral Scientist", 47, 808-827.

[24]*Worthington*, E. L. Jr. (Ed.). (2005a). *Handbook of forgiveness.* New York: Brunner-Routledge.

[25] Worthington, E. L. Jr. (2006). *Forgiveness and reconciliation: Theory and application.* New York: Brunner-Routledge

[26] Worthington Jr, E.L, Witvliet, CVO, Pietrini, P. and Miller, AJ "*Forgiveness*, Health, and Well-Being: A Review of Evidence for Emotional Versus Decisional Forgiveness, Dispositional Forgivingness, and Reduced Unforgiveness". J Behav Med (2007) 30:291–302

[27] Worthington, E. L. Jr. (2001). "Unforgiveness, forgiveness, and reconciliation in societies." In R. G. Helmick & R. L. Petersen (Eds.), *Forgiveness and reconciliation: Religion, public policy, and conflict transformation* (pp. 161–182). Philadelphia: Templeton Foundation Press.

[29] Toussaint, L. L., & Williams, D. R. (October, 2003). "Physiological correlates of forgiveness: Findings from a racially and socioeconomically diverse sample of community resident.

[28] Worthington Jr, E.L, Witvliet, CVO, Pietrini, P. and Miller, AJ "Forgiveness, Health, and Well-Being: A Review of Evidence for Emotional Versus Decisional Forgiveness, Dispositional Forgivingness, and Reduced Unforgiveness." J Behav Med (2007) 30:291–302

[29] Lawler KA, Younger JW, Piferi RL, Jobe, RL, Edmondson, KA, Jones, WH. "The unique effects of forgiveness on health: an exploration of pathways." Journal of Behavioral Medicine, April 2005.

[30] Karremans JC, Van Lange PA, Holland RW. "Forgiveness and its associations with prosocial thinking, feeling, and doing beyond the relationship with the offender." Personality and Social Psychology Bulletin, October 2005.

[31] Dawson. J (1998). *What Christians Should Know About Reconciliation,* Published by international

[32] (President Lincoln gave warning in his proclamation of March 30. 1863)

www.ingramcontent.com/pod-product-compliance
Lightning Source LLC
LaVergne TN
LVHW050024080526
838202LV00069B/6907